The Songwriter's Voice

Conversations with Contemporary Artists

Jane Eamon

Manor House

The Songwriter's Voice

Library and Archives Canada Cataloguing in Publication

Eamon, Jane
    The songwriter's voice : conversations with contemporary artists / Jane Eamon.

ISBN 978-1-897453-36-0

    1. Lyricists--Canada--Interviews. 2. Eamon, Jane. I. Title.

ML423.E125 2012   782.42164'0268   C2012-907730-5

Published November 15, 2012: Manor House Publishing Inc., 452 Cottingham Crescent, Ancaster, ON, CANADA, L9G 3V6 905-648-2193 wwww.manor-house.biz

Cover Design: Donovan Davie based on original art created and supplied by Valzan/Shutterstock

 We acknowledge the financial support of the Government of Canada through the Canada Book Fund (CBF) for our publishing activities.

Note to Reader:
This book is a series of conversations with many songwriters. Generally I start the conversation with a little bit of my own story then I let the writers talk. Once in a while, I'll interject something into the conversation, my thoughts that seem to fit at that moment. When this happens, my words will be in italics.
- Jane Eamon

For Songwriters everywhere
May you always create
And live your dreams

Table of Contents:

THE SONGWRITER'S VOICE

Introduction

Someone once said that songwriting was like a cheap psychiatrist. It can take the place of a willing listener to our anguish and pain. It can comfort and uplift, filling us with hope, laughter and emotion.

It can provide a realm of possibilities not available in any other art form. It can soothe and make us think, remember things we've forgotten – lost loves, childhood, dreams – all in the space of a few moments.

And it is a joyful experience, once you're done. There is nothing more satisfying than a newly finished song. Many fall into the craft naturally after learning to play an instrument. Others start as poets setting words to music. Some find solace in writing, using songwriting as a way to say what they can't say any other way.

There are as many reasons for it as there are people doing it. But it's in the doing where the power lies.

When I decided to do this book project, I thought a lot about why I had chosen the path of a songwriter. I asked questions to anyone who would take the time to answer me honestly. Questions like – am I dooming myself to a life of poverty by choosing to be a songwriter? Or – can I write without performing? Or – do I have to think about the intended audience when I write a song? Or – does a songwriter always have to be hopeful? I was curious and wanted to learn.

I began to wonder if others went through the same things that I did. Over the years, I've met many wonderful writers from all over North America who have inspired me with their dedication and talent. I thought it might be interesting to see how they felt about these things. So I asked them.

I hoped that by recording these conversations, it would inspire others to pick up the pen, perhaps reflect on their own work, or take the time to examine why songwriting is so gratifying.

When I started writing songs I didn't really have a "songwriter" role model. I was always listening to music and there was Joni Mitchell to aspire to. I don't think I wanted to be Joni when I wrote my first song; I just wanted to see if I could do it. It was exciting and more than a little scary. Of course it wasn't any good but it was the first toe in the water.

I wrote in my basement. Songs about what I was going through at the time, all the teenage-angst stuff like crushes and pretend romance. I recorded on a little Sony cassette deck, writing songs that really didn't make a whole lot of sense what with my limited life experience. I don't remember sharing these with anyone else, perhaps my family but certainly not friends.

I wrote a lot in those early years and it's funny looking back on it now; it was much like writing endless reams of poetry. It just happened to be in musical form.

Perhaps I really wanted to be like Joni Mitchell and write something poetic to a guitar. Perhaps I was looking for a means of self-expression in a house full of painters. It may have been the time – early 1970's – when it was cool to write songs.

But then my friends told me I wasn't any good and I took it to heart. I pawned my guitar and walked away from writing for over 26 years.

But I came back. I vowed never to give it up again. There have been days I struggle and rant at the process, but I know truly, I can't give it up. It's my passion and my life-long learning.

Every step is magical and challenging. I was fortunate to have had a mentor who patiently answered each and every one of these same questions over a three-year period while I struggled with my own journey. He is the catalyst for this book.

This is not a "how-to" book, it's a set of conversations.

I sent these same questions I had asked my mentor to 26 writers and left it up to them to answer what they could. They did – every one. All of the writers in this book are professionals in varying degrees.

Some have had commercial success, some dabble, many have been doing it for years and are still doing it; all had something to say. I am so grateful to the writers who responded with candor and honesty. I thank you all. It is heart-warming knowing I share this love of songwriting with so many.

Jane Eamon
Kelowna, BC

MEET THE WRITERS

Ed Winacott was born in the passenger seat of a '35 Pontiac sedan in the midst of a spring storm on March 26, 1944 (there's a story there). His formative years were spent on an Ontario farmstead...with all that entails....a one room school house education....a drafty farm house sans central heating, electricity, or plumbing, but enough to eat. The songs are entries from his musical journal...the ironies, oddities, stories and news items that have stood out.

Ian Robb is a singer and self-described "writer of old songs". He has been performing at folk clubs and festivals for over 40 years, most notably with Toronto's venerable Friends of Fiddler's Green and internationally-known harmony trio Finest Kind. He is a past winner of a Canadian Folk Music Award, and was honoured with the Friends of Fiddler's Green with the 2003 Estelle Klein Award. www.ianrobb.com.

Jim Moffatt   Think Jim Croce meets Godzilla. Fine, strong vocals with excellent, beautiful guitar work and just a piece of the monster to keep it real interesting. www.reverbnation.com/jimmoffatt and www.jimmoffatt.ca

Joanne Stacey is a performing songwriter, both with her band Sister Girl and as a solo artist. She has had numerous honourable mentions and awards for her songwriting and has a publishing deal in Nashville, TN. The mother of 2 grown children, she currently lives in Revelstoke, BC with her husband, Andrew and 2 shih tzus, Pookie & Max. www.reverbnation.com/joannestacey

KJ Denhert is an award-winning independent singer/songwriter, guitarist and band leader from New York City. KJ performs regularly in New York City, making regular tour stops in the French West Indies, Italy and on festival stages around the world. In 2012 she proudly celebrates a landmark 15-year anniversary with her band and the release of her 10th album entitled Destiny. www.kjdenhert.com

Kristin Sweetland is a Canadian guitarist, singer, songwriter, storyteller, photographer and road warrior. www.kristinsweetland.com

Lorraine Hart, singer/songwriter, worked nearly twenty years in New York, then jumped to the Pacific Northwest's jazz scene for the last sixteen years. She has been a blog writer for the Tacoma News Tribune for seven years and published a book of poetry in 2010. She is currently writing two books and a musical, while still writing songs and recording. Poetry book, There I Had to Go, available through www.watermarkwriters.com

Stephen Fearing is a multi-Juno Award winning singer/songwriter. He lives in Halifax N.S www.stephenfearing.com

Norm Strauss started writing songs 30 years ago while working in the logging camps of Northern BC. Out of those isolated settings came a love for songwriting and performing that has taken him as a concert/recording artist all across Europe, Canada and parts of the USA performing in folk clubs, house concerts and festivals. His latest CD, "12 Track Mind" is available for download at www.normstrauss.com

Shari Ulrich is a veteran songwriter who has produced 7 albums of original songs, winning two Juno awards for her work, and has been a songwriting educator since 1992. www.shariulrich.com

David Essig is an Iconic Canadian roots artist, a legendary singer/songwriter, an amazing slide guitarist, and a brilliant live performer. The Victoria Times-Colonist has called David "one of the finest Blues guitarists and songwriters in the world." www.davidessig.com

Hal Brolund A tireless live performer, ambassador for the uke, and all-round great musician. www.manitobahal.com

Maria Dunn is a Juno-nominated songwriter (www.mariadunn.com) who draws deeply on the folk tradition of storytelling through song. Melding North American roots music with her Scottish-Irish heritage, she celebrates the resilience and grace of "ordinary" people, past and present, as on her fifth independent recording *Piece By Piece* (2012), inspired by women working at a Canadian clothing factory.

Yael Wand Between tending to her family and garden in the Cariboo Mountains of British Columbia, Yael creates music with fluid borders. Fusing the spirit of jazz, old time country and modern influences, her music radiates the joy, simplicity and vitality of mountain life.

Mae Moore is an award winning performing songwriter and environmentalist with major label and indie successes. Currently, she divides her time between writing, touring, teaching songwriting, painting and running her organic farm with her husband. www.maemoore.com

Barry Mathers is a multi-award winning singer/songwriter who has had numerous hits on country radio and Country Music Television in Canada. His music has been featured in movies and television as well as being recorded by artists in Canada and Europe. Barry lives in Kelowna, BC where he owns and operates his recording studio, Redhouse Recording. http://www.mathersmusic.ca

Bruce Madole is a great believer in the song as a very short story – and he loves the power of characters and narrative within a deceptively simple lyric. A devoted student of songwriting, his musical influences include roots, blues, and Celtic music, with an occasional streak of gospel and country.

Jory Nash   **www.jorynash.com**

Eve Goldberg Known for her watercolour voice and solid guitar style, Eve Goldberg is a compelling writer and interpreter whose music spans folk, blues, country, swing, bluegrass, and gospel. A favourite at festivals, folk clubs and concert series across Canada and the U.S, she has released three albums to widespread acclaim. www.evegoldberg.com

Andrew Smith is a songwriter, performer, guitarist and music producer. He is the winner of the prestigious Kerrville Newfolk songwriting competition, and has also won awards as a guitarist and as a music producer. www.andrewsmithmusic.com

Dave Borins A fixture in Toronto's acoustic music community, international touring songwriter/performer, Dave Borins plays a high-tempo rhythm based modern interpretation of folk, blues and rock'n'roll. www.daveborins.com

Rosemary Phelan is a Toronto musician, writer, artisan, registered nurse, and glad survivor. Her music, blog, and other endeavours can be found at rosemaryphelan.com

Linda Grenier is a powerful singer who has become an accomplished songwriter and has released three CDs of original material. Lanark County, Ontario is where Linda Marie plays music and writes her songs along the lines of love, loss and life...mostly with a touch of humour.

Lynn Harrison is a singer/songwriter with a lifelong interest in the intersection of creativity and spirituality. She has written and recorded many songs, performs regularly in and around Toronto, and teaches songwriting as a spiritual practice. www.lynnharrison.ca

Gary McGill is a London, Ontario guitarist, singer, and songwriter who has made his sole living at music since 1976. He has one CD to his credit, "Alien Resident in Waiting" released in 1993. "It took 35 years to find out that Mahavishnu wasn't the way to go. Mark Knopfler, James Taylor, Billy Joel, Paul Simon, and Paul McCartney were the way to go..." www.garymcgill.tk

Ian Thomas With a Juno award, four SOCAN classic awards for Painted Ladies, Right Before Your Eyes, Hold On and Pilot, a UNICEF Danny Kaye Humanitarian award, Juno and Gemini nominations, 15 albums and nearly as many top twenty records later, Ian has now added author to the mix with two novels, Bequest (Manor House 2006) and his latest The Lost Chord (Manor House 2008). www.ianthomas.ca

Chapter 1

Why do we write? Are we the only ones who can experience the feelings our words create?

I wonder why I write. From a very early age I made up songs. I made up stories and often put on plays to entertain the family. I always sang songs. When I learned to play the guitar, it was like a new world opened for me. I had written instrumental pieces on the accordion, but the guitar spoke to a different place within me. It gave me something to hang words on to, like a blank page. Anything I was feeling could be expressed with simple music.

But that wasn't the only reason I did it. I just felt like it was my way of being an artist and that was important in my family. I couldn't paint, at least not very well. But I could write in rhyme and felt I was pretty good at it.

I never expected my songs to go any further than myself and my family. I wasn't really a performer, though I did dabble in musical theatre. But that was different. Songwriting was intimate, mine, personal and therapeutic. It was a way to figure things out.

If I had been a performer first, I don't think I would have cared about writing so much. I am a natural ham, but not really. It's like I can put on a mask and be whatever is needed to perform. But when I write, I can't do that. It's much more visceral.

I was curious about what other writers experienced. There seems to be a compulsion that leads us here, to look at things in an artistic way, not in a "this is my career choice, better make a living" way.

David Borins: Why does one write? Is it for attention? Is it for spiritual release? For money? For respect? Out of a compulsion? For change? For aesthetics? To connect with others?

Ian Thomas: Motivations for all writers and even for the individual will vary. For some of us it is how we learn and think. It is often an outlet for much of what our subconscious processes. As Alfred Hitchcock once informed a method actor having a hard time finding his motivation, "Your cheque is your motivation." So sometimes writing out of necessity is a reality in the material world. A passion for the craft and desire to create whether there is a paycheque or not is a good starting point.

Jory Nash: Now this is a question I can relate to. We write because we have to. We write because it makes us feel better to. We write because it's the best way to express what's going on inside us. We write because we can.

The first duty of the performer is to remember the audience. The first duty of the writer is to remember him or herself. That's the biggest difference I see. One can be both and one can please both thyself and the audience but the fundamental duty is different.

Kristin Sweetland: We write because we are compelled, we write because we love it! We also write because we hate it and because we think we should....and of course, we aren't the only ones who can experience what we write. That is the power of music and poetry. Obviously not everyone is going to get it, but that's ok. I would so much rather my songs profoundly affect few than moderately entertain millions and millions.

Hal Brolund: I write for the same reason I breathe. It is necessary. I don't know why or how I came to be this way but it is necessary.

Shari Ulrich: I write because I can and because I need to. Sometimes that need is because I'm in the midst of some trauma drama, and I use it as a way to process what I'm experiencing. But that's a pretty rare state for me, so generally the need for my own creative and professional pride and that I'll be glad I did it when it's over!

Ian Robb: I think this is a very worthwhile question. Over 40 years ago, I used to sing regularly from the floor at London's Singer's Club where evenings were often hosted by Ewan MacColl and Peggy Seeger. This could be a terrifying experience because Ewan was an opinionated and brilliant man, never slow to a challenge and his feedback often questioned a singer's motive as much as his/her technique. More than once, he forced me to examine why I would get up from my chair and choose to sing a particular song rather than just sit and listen to someone else. It was an invaluable if humbling experience. So I think asking songwriters why they write is really good for those who bother to answer truthfully.

Firstly, any songwriter who declares that "WE write because...." is mistaken. I'm afraid I'm probably not part of that "we". I'm perhaps less a songwriter than a singer who is moved to write from time to time. I might write when and if I see or hear the germ of a good story. I might write when I see a good cause that needs a song. I might write when I think someone needs to be laughed at or taken down a peg or two. I always, always write songs in the hope others will be moved to sing them. I rarely write in the first person, unless as narrator. I never write for my own therapy, for the intellectual exercise or to share my personal problems. I really don't "need" to write songs, though I probably do need to sing.

David Essig: For me it's not about choice. We write because that's what we do. I don't believe that we're in any way exclusive. I think anyone with the desire and a modicum of talent and sensitivity to the human condition can do this. It might not work out as great art, but if it emancipates, even for a moment, just one person, then it was worth it.

You just do what you do. I cannot imagine a life without making music. It's part of life itself for me.

Rosemary Phelan: Poetry is my first love. A really good poem will transport us beyond the words themselves with all their layered meanings, to the deep, silent place in our hearts where we experience the unadulterated magic of life. It restores our sense of awe.

But sometimes when I write, the words come nested in a melody, as if they want to be embodied musically. The melody brings certain qualities to the mix; it's an integral part of the message. For me that's what distinguishes a newly blossoming song from a poem-to-be. Both are powerful gifts, especially when shared. I see every human being as an astonishing miracle; a walking cloud of stars. Each unique voice brings ideas and feelings to life in ways no other instrument or voice can, no matter how many times those ideas have been written about before.

Maria Dunn: I write because I have things to say/sing, stories to share with the listener that I don't hear other people writing about, or I have a different view from what I have heard.

I hope that people connect with the songs I write. That's mostly why I write them. Musically, they may never have heard my songs before they see me perform, but I try to write about ordinary people's lives in my songs. I think that listeners can connect with the people (past or present) that I sing about, whether or not the music is to their taste.

Gary McGill: As a therapy: Songs written are like valves that release a specific toxin for something you're going thru. (Excluding the commercial notions, as my efforts have always been organic.)

As a purpose: I enjoy having "sonic children" as it were, as these efforts find purchase in the ears, minds and hearts of others. I look at their reaction, and I say to myself - "I did that."

Barry Mathers: I write for a couple of reasons. Firstly, because it's part of my job as the main songwriter for the Cruzeros and I make money at it. The other is that writing is therapeutic and fun (once you're done) and can actually produce endorphins which make you feel good.

Jory Nash: I write songs. I'm getting something inside of me out when I do. Once I record them or perform them and someone else hears them then whatever they get from that song (good or bad) is now theirs whether I (or they) like it or not.

And if no one listens to what I write and no one cares and no one likes it then perhaps it's time to look for a different occupation. C'est la vie. I simply write and I'm lucky if enough people come along for the ride by hearing something in my songs that they can make their own. Though the art of performance can also come into play in terms of financial success for the performing songwriter but that's really not the question here is it? Obviously I digress.

Joanne Stacey: I write because thoughts, feelings and words seem to course through my veins to a distinct beat and by capturing this, I feel I am tapping into a holy energy that passes through us all. It helps me to feel connected and gives me an outlet that somehow makes sense to my soul and allows others to know me in an intimate way.

There is such great joy and satisfaction when I finish a new song; it is addictive like a drug. You just want to keep doing it. The act of putting words and music together in such a way that evokes a certain feeling is a powerful thing indeed.

Andrew Smith: Why do I write? Because some music really impacts me and moves me in powerful ways; encouraging me, inspiring me, giving me insight and understanding. When that happens, I feel so thankful that the particular musician that I'm listening to has chosen to do what they do. I feel thankful that they have paid the price to follow their muse into sometimes dark and lonely places, and to bring this music back for us. And then I get this irrational desire to be someone who can also impact people, bless people in the same way.

Ed Winacott: There isn't one reason why I do it. Each creation has its own reasons and life for that matter. I have written songs on demand so to speak….that is for some special purpose…wedding, retirement, memorial…and am always surprised that I can. Most of my songs come at me out of the blue and from left field.

I find that songwriting is my equivalent to keeping a diary or journal. They are a record of what was happening to me and others and how I felt about it. So why should I put that down? To make sense of it all to others? Maybe....or maybe to make sense of it to myself. Some songs have been messages from one side of my brain to the other....things I should have known but somehow didn't. There is also the possibility, especially in songs that are very personal in nature, that songwriting is the coward's way out. To make a statement boldly in song when we fear to make it in person. Are we looking for someone who will recognize us in these songs, nod and say "I understand"?

At any rate, it's too late to turn back now!

Jim Moffatt: My reasons for writing are as plentiful and numerous as my imagination. A better question for me is if I didn't write, what then? How would I handle the thoughts and feelings that I have? How would I share them or even think about them to myself? Every song starts as an idea. Even a bad one, idea that is, could make a great song.

Then there is emotion. So why do I write? I write because I have a thought, it turns into an idea....and I use writing and music to solidify my idea so that I get it. It is a fortunate accident that in my process to understand my world, I now have a song that I can share with others.

Bruce Madole: I expect that like many other songwriters the element of compulsion or necessity is a strong factor, just like breathing out is (generally) an inescapable counterpart to breathing in. But underlying that sense of compulsion there is somewhere a conviction that my own voice has a value and that my own words leave an imprint in the silence that is somehow unique and of value to both God and my fellow human beings. Whether or not it is actually "valued" seems to be a separate question, but the act of creative expression carries an intrinsic value, I think, and it may be a spiritual thing, regardless of one's individual creed.

Lorraine Hart: Where does the writer begin? Perhaps it's in having a need to notice and understand. Writing begins in an observer. I realized the company of storytellers from the beginning of consciousness. Events of the day took on narration as if I was trying to explain life to someone else all the time...and amuse them with it. I didn't invent the stories; I heard them. As Bob Dylan said, "you don't make up songs so much as you find them lying on the side of the road." The word crafting is learned and worked at forever but the spring from which all our stories flow.....and the voices that swing them to us are all part of the Great Mystery.

(Beware....the Great Mystery also has a wicked sense of humour and voracious appetite for a little slap and tickle.)

So we write because we have to....whether as a profession or a passionate pastime. All words will evoke feelings, even if it's just confusion or ennui. Trying to share feelings is the raison d'etre for songs....but everyone will caress the part of the elephant in front of them and read the feelings so.

Isn't everything we've learned just our take on a situation? If we are performers first and foremost, would we see it differently?

For me, the most awkward thing I can think of is having my soulful words fall flat in front of an audience. I'm afraid and always have been that people won't get my particular perspective on the world.

I wondered whether other writers ever felt like that. Did they sense that there could be a chance to lose the audience when trying to convey their "take" on the world? Would we always colour our songs with our views?

Lorraine Hart: I agree that everything we've learned is just our take on the situation....and the willingness to be wrong is a very freeing concept, both for writing and living. As a performer, my take on the same song can be completely different each time, dependent on all the other ingredients in the stew of that moment. We take a limited vocabulary and twelve notes...and the possibilities are endless, intoxicating.

Shari Ulrich: We each have a unique way of expressing what we experience, and those experiences tend to be universal. Our "take" (which I translate to mean our personal way of responding to a situation) is unique, and our expression of it is what gives us our unique voice.

Ian Thomas: Maybe everything we've learned is what hobbles us. Is there such a thing as an original "take" or thought? Therefore is our "take" purely ours or an amalgamation of others' "takes" in a unique enough configuration to hopefully have the appearance of originality? It is impossible to escape influence in a media crazy world and yet the metaphor of lyric can often transcend one's own shallowness. Is that a learned experience or a spiritual one? Interesting question.

Hal Brolund: This is the filter that makes your take on a story unique. If we were to stand by a red café table we each would have a different take on the table. We would have different memories informing it and different scenes in our minds. That is our voice. We all see things differently.

Yael Wand: I love putting multiple meanings into my lyrics. Many times I do this purposefully, but often enough I have come to see additional meanings in my own writing after the fact, or else a listener has found their own interpretation. Like any artist, a songwriter plays many roles: a documenter, an interpreter, a mirror, an analyst, and hopefully a visionary too. I'm often conflicted: the more I write, the more I strive to compose material that other performers can make their own. On the other hand, every performer has her own strengths and weaknesses and style, and I love the idea that as a writer and a performer I am in a privileged position to create material that I can embody and present better than anyone else – material that stems from and resonates with my soul.

Kristin Sweetland: Sometimes I do feel that only I can bring the hidden meanings or that I have something to say, personally and it needs to be both written and spoken by me. In fact, I believe this is what ultimately drives me to perform; to say what only I can. However, I would LOVE to write songs for other performers to sing and believe that a truly brilliant song can be sung by anyone – and it will always be brilliant.

Chapter 2

When did you first ever begin to write songs? How old were you?

I wrote my first song when I was 17. There was a contest to write a song about the county I lived in, so I wrote "Land of Chinguacousy" – a terrible song. I didn't win, but the contest organizers liked the song enough to bring me into a studio to record it. I'll never forget the exhilaration of playing that song into a microphone. Funny, I don't remember writing anything else until I moved to the west coast four years later.

Playing often and with others pushed me to write things outside of my own way of thinking. It was an intense learning time with lots of output. There wasn't a lot of censorship. It didn't matter if the songs were good or not, it was enough I was writing them. I began to play with form and genre because I didn't have a frame of reference for what I should or shouldn't do. I didn't know what I was doing. But I did it anyway.

Was it an "a-ha" moment? I don't know. I do know that it was interesting realizing that I could write a story in rhyme with music and say something. It probably took me a long time to discover what made a good song. But at this point I was just writing about anything.

Ed Winacott: What impelled me to write? What made me think I should or could write songs? As a child I was very aware of the magic and power of words in their sounds, their rhythms, their selection and arrangements to evoke images and emotions and to touch, however briefly, some essential part of being human.

Was I looking for that ability to so move and touch? Maybe. Anyhow, I do know that my songwriting is lyrically driven...at first I didn't even play an instrument. So why not a poet? I have a friend who once described me as a poet who had the misfortune to play the guitar.

Perhaps the answer lies in what I was exposed to musically. Our radio played mainly country songs when I was a child and no matter how you feel about country music, it does appeal to emotions, sometimes rather blatantly and superficially.

I also grew up and came of age in a rich folk era....Leonard Cohen, Gordon Lightfoot, Joni Mitchell, Dylan, Ian and Sylvia and all of those other great songwriters from that time. Songs where the words and the message counted like I felt they should. I found that music with its melody and rhythm when matched in mood and lyrics has a kind of power that words alone struggle to accomplish.....so I got a guitar and learned to play it well enough to serve.

Jim Moffatt: I have written as long as I can remember. I was using paint in the old "paint by numbers" set to paint stories and what I was thinking before I could talk and long before I started to know just what I was doing. I only knew that I had to do it.

As I got older, I began to learn language and music and began to understand that with those I could convey the emotion better than with a picture alone. In grade one I saw a student in my class sing to the whole school a simple sing, "Bicycle Built for Two". I suddenly understood the power of music and song.

Linda Grenier: I was 18 years old when I wrote my first song. I had been playing guitar since I was 10 and I was going through some tough boyfriend times and I just did it. I didn't even think about it.

I had written poems since I can remember, submitting them in contests in public school. I wanted to write a song to incorporate my own music to my poetry so that I could perform it and share it with others.

I do think saying I had no choice might have some validity. But I'm beginning to examine why I started writing in song form and what actually made me think I could AND it would have some worth outside of my basement. Does social environment play a role?

Leaving the discussion of "worth" out of the equation (that's a whole other can of worms) I would say that from an early age I listened to the radio and was always impressed by how a song made me feel. At the age of 7, Neil Young's, "Heart of Gold", made me want to play guitar and harmonica at the same time, way before I even had a guitar. I have always been in awe of music, no matter what genre. It fascinates me that such music can come out of the soul and mind.

David Essig: I was about 18 when I wrote the first song that I could really be comfortable with performing in front of other people. I wrote it about a real-life situation and it made me feel great. I still perform that song.

Looking over all these years, I'd say the difficulties of life more often caused me to pick up the pen than to put it down. The years when I was in public office were very distracting and I didn't get a lot of writing done then – one of the reasons I left that work and returned full-time to music.

Norm Strauss: I first started learning to play guitar in earnest when I was 19 years old. I was working in the winter logging camps of Northern BC and in the evenings I had nothing to do so I bought a Yamaha guitar and had a little cassette player. I spent hours trying to figure out the finger-picking patterns of James Taylor, Noel Paul Stookey and Mark Heard. I didn't actually start writing songs until I was 22 years old. I moved down to the Okanagan to go to college and I met a guy named Marty Perrin who was a few years older than me but at the same college. He was the first singer/songwriter I had ever met in person and I was a bit in awe of his ability to tell stories and make brand new songs just with his guitar and voice. He encouraged me to start writing and we ended up doing a few coffeehouse concerts together. I have a cassette bootleg copy of our first concert someone recorded. I probably should destroy it because it would be awful if it ever got out in public.

My first song I wrote was ironically titled "A Simple Song". It was a gentle folk song that was about 8 verses long and talked about everything I thought I knew about God, philosophy, politics and science. I took me about 10 minutes to sing it and the verses were preachy and scattershot. I remember feeling incredulous that I had actually completed a song. The chorus went "This is my song and I'm singing it for all of you. I'll sing it as sweetly as I can. The words are simple 'cause I'm only a simple man. Still I'd like to sing my song for you." Very sappy. Marty's comment was, "You need to go out and live some life before you write about all those topics."

Anyways, it never became a hit song of course but it did unlock something because for the next 5 years or so I wrote on average 2-3 songs a week. Literally hundreds of songs most of which were never recorded and are now lost somewhere in the mists. Nine out ten of those songs were pretty uninspired anyways but I did manage to develop some chops during that time.

Joanne Stacey: Well, I probably started writing songs before I realized that I was doing it. When I was 11, I wrote my first "real" song with 2 verses and a chorus, which was written vocally, full melody and lyrics. It was pretty sappy and I laugh now when I think about it because I still remember how to sing the chorus. I remember feeling so elated when I sang it! And so free! Like I was some sort of superhero and I would sing it when I walked to school and when I was alone at home. I don't think I ever shared it with anyone, except one of my friends that I grew up with.

Jane Eamon: I think that encouragement of any kind at this early stage of my writing really shaped the way I worked at it. I felt like I was part of something very special, even though to tell you the truth, I could only name one female singer/songwriter that I knew of. I wasn't trying to emulate anyone but myself, but all of my experiences with musical theatre and music I listened to while growing up, helped me to form my own songs. I was not an accomplished guitar player but it was enough that I knew a few chords and could strum along while I sang.

Chapter 3

What are you when you write? A musician? A poet? A dramatist? A performer? What hat do you wear when you write and perform?

Of course we are writers. But sometimes we are more than that. We unconsciously wear the hat of a musician, a performer, a poet and an actor. If we choose to sing our own material, we have to portray it in the best way possible. So the actor takes over. Giving the most emotional and authentic performance we can to convey the emotions and meanings of our words.

But personally, I try to strive for the poetry of the words. Even though I'm very aware of the limited space I have to share those words, it's so important to be able to say EXACTLY what I need to say in that moment. Words become so vital to the message. Without the right words, I waste time and space with the wrong things. I am not always successful with this, so the dramatist in me needs work. I find I settle too often for words that fit sort-of and at least get the song finished.

I was a newbie at performance. I have so much baggage attached to my performance skills. I constantly measure myself against those I admire. And that's death. I will never be them; I will never be the best. There will always be someone younger, faster, smarter, more technically advanced, fill in the blank. But I am getting better, I'm starting to like my style and accept it whatever shape it takes. So in that sense, I'm learning how to be a performer.

But I think there is a place for me and my music. It takes courage and strength to keep going no matter what and accept whatever comes, no matter what.

Jory Nash: In the words of Bob Dylan, I'm just a song and dance man, which is to say that I have NO IDEA what I am when I write. I write because I like to. I write because I want to. I don't write because I don't want to. If someone calls me a poet, am I one if another person says my stuff is unpoetic? I don't know what those labels mean. I guess I am just what people see me as, nothing more, nothing less.

As for what hat I wear when I perform...that's easy; whatever hat I pull out of the box that night. I have hundreds of hats, literally. All kidding aside, I understand this question more than the first one. My role as a performer is to entertain....people have paid good money to come see me play and I'd damn well better entertain them, even if I'm not in the mood to do so. So it's part actor, part inspired artist, part megalomaniac. And if I'm real good, I'll sell some CDs and make some money from my songwriting.

Kristin Sweetland: I am sometimes a musician first and sometimes first a writer – it is when these two personas meet and agree that I know I have something!

Yael Wand: There are many ways I write. First and foremost I am human and I try to embody some human emotion or a specific perspective when I write. I don't try to reach everybody with one particular song, but if I can relate to the emotion or thought than I know somebody else will too – maybe only one person, maybe many more. So when I write I am a humanist. When it comes to crafting a moving song, I can use many techniques – perhaps I embody a particular character, or I place the character in a specific setting with imaginary sights, sounds, smells or tastes. Sometimes the character is me, but most often I embellish my own circumstances so that the perspective in the song is fuller, richer and far more interesting than me. A listener once approached me and applauded me for writing so personally and truthfully. I couldn't convince him that my songs didn't stem from personal experiences but were embellishments of my reality or elaborated on by my imagination.

Shari Ulrich: I don't think I have a hat! To me that sounds like having a voyeur in the room who will judge and edit and get in the way of the creative process or the performance. I've never analyzed it, but I think I am simply a translator of being human into song.

Andrew Smith: If it brings me joy and satisfaction, it is probably connected with music and art. So I'm happy to wear other hats and to work other "jobs" in the big wide world of music besides writing and performing such as producing and doing session work. It helps pay the bills and I enjoy it, though writing and performing is my favourite part of being a musician.

Mostly when I write songs with lyrics, I write as a craftsman and a storyteller. I want to tell a story well. I want the listener to be transported into the scene – to *see* the scene and to *feel* an emotional connection with what's being described.

Occasionally the songs come less deliberately, more stream of consciousness, more poetic. I think this is particularly true when I write instrumental music.

Barry Mathers: I try and get a scenario going in my head about the song, kind of like watching a movie. I usually reflect back on a situation and just write about it. I find it easier to write about real things than to make something up. What hat do I wear? My cowboy hat.

Ian Thomas: In songwriting one often performs in the writing process while dramatizing a story in poetic or lyrical terms. Lyrics can be dramatic, tell stories or manifest in more impressionistic poetry through metaphor. Once again there are no absolutes and often the way to find a song can be through any of these means or in combination.

David Essig: I'd say "storyteller" pretty well sums it up for me – especially as a performer. When I'm in that solitary moment of writing, I often view myself as "film director", picking the shots and lining them up to tell the story. I'd like to be remembered as a poetic storyteller who played the guitar.

Maria Dunn: I think I am all of these things at different stages in the songwriting process. It depends on the song I'm writing and why I'm writing it. If I'm writing a commissioned song for an organization or individual or a historical song about a specific event, my first role is a researcher. I read up on/get to know the organization/individual through attending events, meeting with people in the organization. I listen to oral history, sometimes with individuals, sometimes with a group. What do they want to hear in a song that they've commissioned, what are the important themes, events, emotions that they want to get across? I synthesize these ideas, themes and the purposes of the song. What style of music will best fit these themes, this story? I check in with the song commissioner, does this song ring true? Then I make requested changes if I am able to.

If I am writing a historical song, I immerse myself in the period by "reading around" a historical event, reading as much as possible about the original event (history books, memoirs, archives, oral history interviews). I talk to/listen to the people who were there (obviously more recent events). I try to find the emotional kernel of the song, why do I want to tell this story? Why is it important? Why should anyone care? I try to find the balance between telling the history (dates, names, accuracy of events) and make the song poetic.

Sometimes the music comes first, as I'm getting myself in the spirit of the period or event; sometimes I hash it out once the lyrics are there (in which case the lyrics tend to establish a natural rhythm from which to work the music out).

If the song is about a person, real or fictional, present or historical, and I am presenting the character as "first person", then there definitely is an element of the dramatist involved. I try to get into that character's skin. It's an excellent opportunity to work with language that would be true to that character and that period (as in the case of "God Bless Us Everyone" that I wrote from the point of view of Tiny Tim Cratchit in Dickens' "A Christmas Carol") but not true to me personally.

As I polish the songs up and think about how to arrange them for live performance, then I put on my performer hat and start to make changes based on imagining how something will work in a concert setting.

Sometimes the performer hat comes on earlier if the song is for a specific purpose – a labour rally, for instance – then I might think earlier in the songwriting stage about how I can engage the audience in joining in on a chorus or how I might write a more call-and-response song to make it more easily communal.

Mae Moore: I am almost always in a state of inner reflection when I write and therefore tapping into my own subconscious awareness. Since I write almost exclusively in alternate tunings, this process is guided by whatever tuning I stumble upon and the inherent chords that go along with it. It could be a very minor modal tuning that picks the subject path (usually pathos), the melody follows and the lyrics launch from there. I don't think of myself as anything in particular, but am open and follow the inner voice. I usually wear a handmade knitted hat when I perform, but have been seen in a crushed velvet one from time to time.

KJ Denhert: I like to write melodies and always have – once I try to connect that to chord progressions and arrangements, I feel most like a musician and I work at it – singing, revising and improvising. I have a real penchant for performance. Performing is the easiest part of the whole thing for me – it's so validating to have the opportunity to perform that I feel successful regardless. I imagine performing the songs as I write them but lately I have been writing with a friend I made in Hamburg, most of the songs have been intended for her upcoming release but I get so into it that I start performing them on my own.

Hal Brolund: When I perform, I am a performer. I am open to the moment of entertaining. Being funny, charming, sly, creepy, happy, whatever to move the show forward. I am this way regardless of whether the songs I sing are mine or not. When I write though, I am thinking only of the song and its story. I am wearing the hat of storyteller first here and entertainer second.

Ian Thomas: One who views performance as their passion could view the song simply as a means to an end. But the song often is the "end" for the writer. Performers and writers can often have a symbiotic relationship. A motivation to perform can be a creative motivation. What a blessing that Pavarotti had such wonderful arias to sing. For the writer of the aria, how wonderful there are voices such as Pavarotti to sing them.

Lorraine Hart: Movement is the key....to writing and living in a universe that never stays still. I (only half-jokingly) always refer to my "312 personalities" and dance between them. You cannot be all things...but you can let all things run through you and choose for your writing what is relevant for the story you're trying to tell.

One of the best pieces of advice I was ever given about writing songs was to think "little movies", if the song is a story. Sometimes, rather than a little movie it can be a painting or sculpture...words as texture and mood instead of narration.

You can reflect on all the things you have an emotional connection to. But try to write something with false connections and you'll convince no one. That doesn't mean to say you can't write to order, professionally; you just have to find your connection and begin from there.

I prefer to think of shape-shifting rather than hats. It gives more of the motion from inside to out and implies something deeper that a costume change. My spirit must be present and constant to facilitate a song and performance that takes both audience and performer to that different place....and return satisfied.

For me, first the Muse writes something. Then, as a journeyman-musician-poet-dramatist-craftsman-performer I work it...and rework it as I see how it flies in performance. The secret is to leave enough room in your story for your audience to feel their own story within, in whatever way and character their multiple personalities connect to.

Artists balance between beacon and mirror to serve society and satiate their own constant calling from the simplest escape of entertainment to the most complex connection of co-creation.

Jane Eamon: This is an interesting conversation about what we are when we write. If you break it down into little pieces, it's more than just the writing. It's also the shaping of the delivery, acting the parts, playing the music and writing the content. That's a plateful! And we do it so naturally. I don't think I've ever really thought about what "hat" I wear when I do certain parts of it. I just do it and it all seems to come together.

Chapter 4

Do we write to please ourselves or with others in mind, writing for an intended audience as opposed to just writing?

I have a fear of the audience. I'm not comfortable singing in front of them though I do it a lot. If I were to write thinking about who was going to hear it, I wouldn't be able to finish let alone start. But if I have to write a song for a specific purpose, I have to think about my audience. I do write a lot of songs about me. They are after all, my diaries.

But I think it's a valid question. Sometimes songs we write to please ourselves are not fit for mass consumption. They are too personal. We do have to stay true to our authentic selves in order to write well. Of course, you can craft a story that has no connection to you personally. There are a lot of great songwriters who do this all the time. But it's not as easy as it seems. A well-crafted story song is just as important as a piece of fiction. It requires the same depth of skill and technique not to mention writing it in rhyme and under 10 minutes!

If I were a Nashville writer-for-hire, the intended audience would be on my mind always. Who's going to sing the song? Will it get picked? Then the song becomes an object, not a personal reflection though the truth still has to be there. We cannot write well when the audience cannot connect to what we say. So there's the conundrum. Keep the audience at bay while writing OR think about them in some way depending on the subject material.

Lynn Harrison: I see myself as the first person I need to please…but I'm always conscious that I want my songs to be useful to others. To please both myself and anybody else, I need to make sure my songs are sensible and clear and interesting. It's a matter of respect for whoever's listening. For me that includes God or The Patterning Intelligence that Makes All Songs Possible. I try not to worry much about which particular people might be listening (or how many they may be). I say "try" because of course I have found myself worrying at times (after the song is finished) about who's listening to it or approving of it. Increasingly though, I believe that such an evaluation is imperfect at best (who really knows who's listening or what they think?) and that focusing on imaginary audiences distracts me from my more pressing goal, which is to write a good song. If I do that, I find there's an audience for it. Might not be the one I expect, but there's an audience.

KJ Denhert: I believe that if someone paid money to come and see me, I have a responsibility to entertain him or her, they don't owe me anything. People are inspired by real emotion. I try to animate the music and lyrics with everything that I have – my face, movement, my hair, dancing. Sometimes it's painful to watch the video – it always feels so much more graceful from inside of me than what I see on camera. I just have to let go of trying to appear cool (the greatest temptation BTW) and be unabashed. That took many years to really internalize. It sounds a lot easier than it is to truly accomplish. It's a classic ego struggle. I even created my own little prayer asking for my ego to be put aside before I get in front of an audience.

To play well I have to be very strict – don't try to impress anyone I tell myself. It's hard when an agent or promoter comes to a show because you want the work – but for me – it's the only way. It probably looks like I'm ignoring their presence. One last good trick is to open your eyes, smile and make eye contact now and then. People love that, it's infectious – unless of course they hate what you're doing. If you think someone really doesn't like what you're doing, don't make too much eye contact if at first you feel nothing. When that happens I just listen to the virtual record I'm creating on the spot. Sure sometimes you just have an off night but you should never start out just playing for yourself – that's a last resort that I abhor.

I believe that truth enables Dharma. With that said how one interprets their truth is still open to quite a bit of interpretation. Art is about the things that don't have words. I believe that there is a tasteful way to approach the truth – Ozzy Osbourne could say the same I'm sure. For example I bet he never wanted his songs to sound wimpy or timid. I don't want to sound wimpy or timid either.

Maria Dunn: I firmly believe that you need to write some of those deeply personal songs to express the emotion, if only to yourself. I think it's important though, to recognize that some songs would be better **not shared** with a listening/concert audience. Or take that emotion, write your personal version and then take a step back and put your editor's hat on and figure out if there's a way to make it more universal, so that your audience can connect with it and that you are not baring your soul for the sake of baring your soul, but that you've written a good song that people can relate to.

Joanne Stacey: Unless I have been commissioned to write a song for a particular reason, I never write to please anyone but myself. It is a deeply personal place that I allow myself to go to; where I can connect with the Muse to create the song it has placed within me to write. Once it is completed, I look at it and decide whether it is a song I will sing to others or not. Only then do I consider the audience.

Ian Thomas: One doesn't necessarily exclude the other; however, the most satisfying experience for me is music I have written for self. Perhaps the most any of us has to offer is how light might shine through one's particular prism as unfettered by conscious influences as possible. But, I have also found great satisfaction in creating music for a specific project or audience.

Jory Nash: No, but I do have the audience in my mind's eye when I perform. Some songs might be inappropriate for certain audiences. I have a few friends in the Catholic Church. If they come and see me play I avoid two overt anti-God songs I have and concentrate more on the questioning of God songs I have.

Writing songs can be looked at like giving birth. I imagine a birth mother is in such pain and under such intense focus that she's not thinking of much else except giving birth at that very moment. For me, songwriting elicits a similar focus. Once the tune is done then I can think about the audience. But they have no place in my songwriting process and I couldn't think about them even if I wanted to.

Hal Brolund: Here's the rub and quite possibly there are many who would disagree but I think that we need to plumb the depths to create a story that is authentic and will speak to the hearts and minds of the listener. I don't specifically mean that we need to write every story of our own life but we need to be able to use the filter of our life to give a story meaning. We need memories of being snowed in to write "Bob was snowed in" and give it real meaning and authenticity. The listener knows when the story isn't authentic. It's the editor who decides what was for personal growth and what is a compelling public story.

Kristin Sweetland: I think some of us write to please ourselves and some of us write to try and please others. I guess it depends on what gives you the most satisfaction – to think you are brilliant or to have someone else think you are brilliant. Obviously a combination of both would be nice....

Shari Ulrich: I LOVE the feeling when it works – it can be so exciting. But no, I'm not thinking about the audience at the moment – I'm pleasing myself and then I can't wait to share it with others.

David Borins: I think writing often happens without regard for other's opinions. The creation of the piece excites the writer. When it comes down to performance and presentation, there is a give and take that is essential to the success of the person on stage. Unless the performer falls into the category of "I'm absolutely undeniably amazing so I have the liberty of ignoring you, the paying audience", I'm fairly certain the audience will be kept in the loop.

Norm Strauss: Part of the skill of a writer, of a healthy person period, is to intuitively know what is worth communication and what isn't. This kind of filtering is not a sin, and it doesn't mean we don't write honestly and with self-disclosure or that we can't spill our guts when we write. It just means that we are skilled communicators and recognize ourselves as participants in the rest of humanity. Also, sometimes you write a song that is just for you and your mother to hear. Or maybe just you (maybe your mom has some other stuff to do today). Maybe some songs you write are meant to be therapeutic for you, but don't find resonance with many other people. That's ok, keep writing those songs. They are worth just as much as any other song.

You are a member of the human race first of all (some songwriters can seem like aliens I know). Songwriting is one of the ways you communicate. I do believe that you are to write from the depths of your psyche, but the truth is that sometimes your fellow man doesn't really care to know what some parts of your inner psyche are saying. Or maybe you are saying it in a boring way. Also I have met some songwriters that seem to be needy people emotionally. Their songs tend toward excessive amounts of self-absorption and become draining to listen to as well, just as if you were having conversations with that person on a regular basis.

Jane Eamon: I agree that one of the universal truths of songwriting is the desire to connect it to the human experience. We start out writing from and about our own experiences. For me, it was what I saw and how I felt about it. They were my impressions and I knew them intimately. I tried to communicate them to others who perhaps by hearing my words could share my experience.

I sometimes wonder why I have to share my observations with others. Is that the mark of a writer? This compelling need to express in song what I see? I think that's part of it. It's a little storyteller but it's a little reporter too. I wanted to make sense for myself what I experienced and by doing so, maybe clear the way for someone else to come to understand things in their own life. It's cathartic. It gets it out of me. It's like that bug in its case, you can always put it away when you're done looking.

David Essig: I try to keep Roland Barth's notion of the "model reader," at hand when I'm writing. I have an imaginary "model listener," that I write for.

Mae Moore: I like to work in solitude so thinking about the audience makes me feel uncomfortable.

Chapter 5

Writing without performing, is it possible?

When I first started writing songs I was terrified of performing. I didn't want to get on stage and share my stuff for fear of being rejected. Rejection is a powerful deterrent and I did not want to set myself up to deal with that.

But I was on fire writing songs. I wanted to find out if I could write and do it well without having to sing the songs. Would someone else sing them for me? I knew nothing about the "business" of writing for others. But in hindsight, it was a coward's move. I was afraid to get on that stage and sing my own songs.

I know now there are a lot of great writers that have made a good living writing without performing. They have no desire to perform, why should they? They write the songs, someone else sings them, they get paid.

Seemed like an easy way for me to do this writing thing. Little did I know that eventually I wanted to sing my own songs, however immature they were. I wanted to share MY story. Maybe that's the actor in me; I wanted to be on that stage without fear of singing my stuff. Besides what was the worst that could happen? Nobody liked my stuff? Wow….never once did I get booed off the stage.

I was curious to see how the other writers dealt with this. A lot of them are excellent performers as well as songwriters.

Hal Brolund: Is it possible to write without performing? It had better be.

Kristin Sweetland: Yes yes! Of course.

Shari Ulrich: I can't quite separate being a writer from being a performer as performance is just the delivery of what I write.

Barry Mathers: Absolutely. I don't perform everything I write. Some songs are performed by other artists and some just aren't suitable for the live show.

Jory Nash: EXCELLENT question!!! But I can't answer it. I simply don't know. I've only ever written AND performed. Not either/or. My guess is no…simply because even if I just write and play it to one friend privately that would be considered a performance.

Lorraine Hart: I like writing songs for other people as well, allowing me a wide range of genres to play in. After the initial umbilical whiplash, I can appreciate the different energy and meaning another voice can put into a piece I wrote subjectively. That refers again to the "room" inside a song's lyrics for the listener (or another interpreter) to put in their own stories and emotions. My wish as a performer of my own material is that you get to check out the original. My wish as a songwriter is that the songs go on without me. My wish is that they have a life of their own, long after I'm gone from this place.

KJ Denhert: Everything is possible – I really have just begun to internalize how much we create our own reality. It's soooo darn liberating. I started writing at 10 because I was moved by the idea of a teacher dying – there was no performance plan but soon my friends were coming over after school and I would play my one song.

Ian Robb: If you (the impersonal "you") are a songwriter first and a singer second, it's easy to jump to the conclusion that perhaps you are writing for other singers as much as yourself. But perhaps you (still impersonal) are writing songs mainly because you derive gratification or therapy or some other value from the "process" regardless of whether the results are sung or not. In which case, they really need to be focused on your own particular personal experience without having to worry about writing for other singers. Or I guess, the audience.

I suspect that the reality lies somewhere between these two simplistic scenarios. My impression – and it is just that – is that for many professional singer/songwriters, the singing and the writing are symbiotic and inseparable. One is not more important than the other. That's why they are called singer/songwriters. As for me, I can – and do – take or leave my own songs in performance. There are lots of other great songs to sing. My only compulsion to sing my own is so that someone else will like them enough to sing them, which is ultimately why I write them. But for me performance as a whole – the singing – comes before even that consideration.

David Essig: Except for a couple of film gigs, this is not possible for me. I really need the feedback from the audience to see where a song is heading – where a body of work is heading. I'm thinking fine-tuning here – watching the audience react to certain turns of phrase, certain language, the way the songs weave together over a performance, and making microscopic changes to make the work more accessible to the listeners.

Lynn Harrison: There as a long period of my life (from about 13 to about 34) when I wrote many songs but did not perform publicly. I expect that later in life I will continue to write even though I may or may not perform. Recently I have been visiting a 90-year–old woman in my neighbourhood who is (still) a very highly accomplished pianist. Expertly trained in St. Petersburg as a child and continuing to develop her significant skill throughout her life, she did not have the opportunity to become a professional musician, working instead as a housekeeper and a nurse. The fact that music did not – ever – play a professional role in her life in no way diminishes its importance to her or the depth of her personal accomplishment. Especially as she has grown older and has become more isolated, she sees music as the most meaningful activity in her life – a pathway to truth and beauty and serenity even as her body fails her. She maintains exceptionally high standards for her playing even though she plays "only" for herself. In fact, she does not simply play "to herself". She (consciously) plays to Life. To God. To Music itself.

Maria Dunn: I believe it is possible to write without performing although I've never tried writing for another performer yet. I imagine you would have to be reasonably functional on voice or another instrument to get your musical ideas across (so at least "performing" for your cat) but there's no reason I can think as to why you have to perform to be able to write.

Shari Ulrich: I don't think I'd want to. I suppose that's because I was a musician before I was a writer or singer so performing is such a big part of the joy of music for me. But of course there are thousands of great writers who write and don't perform and have no interest. Performing for me is the payoff for writing the songs and the point of delivery for the words I want to share.

David Borins: I guess the majority of songwriters who make a living at it, fall into this category. It's a job like any other, particularly in Nashville. Would I do it? Yes and no – I'd be thrilled if others want to pay me to use things I've written, but I find so much joy in performing that I will do it even if it's just a secondary hobby. If one day, I wake up and say, I'm tired of this whole music thing, I'm heading back to school to be an accountant, I'd probably inadvertently write songs about accounting and perform then at the campus pub.

Ian Thomas: Non-performing writers remain a huge part of the music business. Writing may very well be the joy while the rest of it can be a monumental pain in the ass. Some of the best songwriters in history have made wonderful livings without the horrors of fame and celebrity.

Andrew Smith: It's possible as long as SOMEONE performs it.......

Mae Moore: My lawyer, upon the signing of my deal with Sony, asked me if I really wanted to be out on the road touring for years and years. He said, "Wouldn't you rather just write the songs and have other people perform them?" With the spirit of youth, I answered, "No, I want to perform. I can do this." Being away from home for extended periods of time took its toll on the relationships that I was in at this time. I missed the weddings of close friends, the births of children, many things. Would I have done things differently? Maybe....if you look at someone like Jim Vallance who has written scores of multimillion selling songs, it is doable. It's a lifestyle choice.

Lorraine Hart: This is a question that hits me where I live right now. Being my adult daughter's caregiver and having some dental issues have cut back my performing schedule in the last few years. At the same time, I'm writing more than I ever have. It's hard to look at the possibility of writing without performing....but it's impossible to think of not writing.

Chapter 6

Singing the songs of others and not your own

Early in my career as a singer/songwriter I realized that not ALL of my own songs were successful in a concert setting. Sometimes they were too long, not clear enough, poorly executed on guitar, missing elements, fill in the blank.....there are so many reasons why a song doesn't work. Since I was trying so hard to find my own identity as a writer, I was reluctant to sing other people's songs. I wanted to explore my own writing and try and figure out why things weren't working.

I have great respect for other songwriters. I admire and feel blessed when someone writes a good song. It's only been recently that I've been able to sing their songs with conviction because I've travelled that path. I know how hard it is to write a good song. And I feel comfortable enough now to be able to let someone else's emotions and story come through me, my voice.

Performance is not my first love, perhaps if it was; I would have enjoyed singing someone else's songs for the sake of the show. But I was trying to get myself sorted out. I wanted to be known as a writer not just a performer. So in the blindness of not knowing any better, I sang my own material almost exclusively. I didn't care whether anyone liked it or not, though actually I did. And I grew as a writer. It was my trial by fire.

But I did learn how to ask for feedback from people I admired. And I listened. I didn't always follow their advice, but I listened. It really helped.

Perhaps the key is not taking oneself too seriously.

Jory Nash: I look at my songs like paintings. Everyone, including myself will see/hear different things in them. If someone else wants to sing my songs, go ahead. I might not like what I hear but I don't for a second believe I have the only key to my songs. I like to perform other people's songs. Mostly songs by dead people and writers I will never meet. That way they can't tell me my versions of their songs are shit. No, I play (and record) other people's songs because I like other people's songs and it makes for a more interesting performance. For me and for the audience. And no artist has created their art in a vacuum; something had to come before to inspire them. Homage is important where art is concerned.

Maria Dunn: I love singing other people's songs too. I mostly sing my own songs when I perform a concert because that is usually why I'm being hired. Sometimes I'll work a traditional song or two into the show, if I'm not rushed for time. With 3 CDs of my own songs and another on the way, I have too many of my own songs that I can't fit into a standard concert set. Unfortunately the economics of the music business mean that, if I only have a certain # of songs to sing and I spent X amount of dollars recording and manufacturing my CDs, plus Y amount of dollars shipping them to the place I'm performing, then I'm going to make my own songs a priority. So other people's songs are saved for special occasions, or music jams, and then they are a delight to pull out!

Barry Mathers: I perform my own songs because that's how I make my living. I have also been fortunate to have other artists such as country singer Julian Austin record songs I have written. I enjoy performing songs written by other songwriters, but I have to really like them. I always throw in some cover tunes as well because people enjoy hearing something familiar amidst a bunch of songs they haven't heard before.

David Essig: I perform the songs I write because those are the kinds of songs I like to hear. (I'm borrowing from Alice Munro who says she writes the kind of stories she likes to read.) I enjoy singing the songs, telling the stories, playing the guitar and experiencing the "ah-ha" from the audience when they get it.

KJ Denhert: I sing other artists' songs, usually hit songs and I am incredibly honoured when someone sings my songs.

I heard one of my songs recently recorded by Nicole Henry and I just loved it. I felt suspended in a magical place as I listened. It was as though I knew what was coming but every detail was different.

Ian Robb: I try very hard to apply the same criteria to my own songs as I do to those of other writers, known or anon. I may not completely live up to that ideal – like all writers I do have an ego – but I'm generally pretty reluctant to sing my own songs unless I feel they stand up to the rest of my repertoire and will mean as much to my audience.

Hal Brolund: I started performing my own songs because I didn't sound like anyone else when I was playing. I would perform an Eric Clapton song and not sound anything like him but instead sound like me. So I started just skipping the middle man and singing a song that came from me and sounded like me.

David Essig: Some listeners seem to find significance in my work; others are mystified. I actually have two audiences: the songwriter audience that tends to immerse itself in the words, the images, the stories and the guitar audience that comes for the hot licks. To the latter I like to say, come for the guitar but stay for the songs and many of them have.

Lynn Harrison: I believe that when we write with originality and insight that communicates clearly to the audience (that is, when our songs are beautiful and truthful because they're built on excellent melody, structure and lyrics) then the level of applause will likely be higher, because it's clear we've done something difficult to do. The audience has witnessed a feat of some daring and skill…which is worth clapping for! That said, a faithful rendition of any beautiful song is a wonderful thing….and when you play a cover you give the audience the thrill of recognizing and appreciating a song they already know and love. Either way, the key is that the song be excellent…which is to say beautiful and meaningful.

Yael Wand: I think I've grown an invisible layer of skin over the years that I have been performing. I can stand in front an audience of hundreds and disclose extremely intimate details by means of a song and for the purpose of the song. On the other hand, there's a mental preparation for doing so… when I've been called upon all of a sudden to perform, and especially when I perform in front of those closest to me, I feel utterly naked, that invisible skin is gone. My best gigs are for strangers because we start at the same point, as strangers, and we get to know each other at the same time: me reading their response, them reading my performance. And still, there is no one that reads my lines as closely as my mother, and there are no bigger fans of mine than my family. Go figure.

Shari Ulrich: Years ago, when I was just a musician and singer, before I wrote my own songs, I was uncomfortable singing other people's words, because they simply weren't my own. They didn't fit me very well. That was my main impetus to write. I play the songs I write because we tend to write for our own voices and there is a depth and subtlety in expression that I do believe brings an extra dimension to a song. But not every writer is the best interpreter of their songs!

I think people respond to me because the essential consciousness when I'm performing a song: a sense of gratitude that this was "given" to me – both the gift of the song and the voice to sing it becomes a shared celebration of the power of music and the joy it brings into our lives and that focus is what prevails – not "look at me".

David Borins: When it comes down to choosing material to perform, it's all about context and execution. Applause is easy to come by...ask anyone who has played "Hey Jude" or a slowed-down version of a rap song in a crowded bar. Gaining an audience's respect is more difficult and generally can't be found without gimmicks in a party first, music second setting. You are most likely to be applauded with respect in a listening environment (theatre, coffee shop, etc.) from material executed expertly, uniquely and with passion. In a live setting, you are the author of the performance, the song's writer is secondary, just ask Elvis.

Andrew Smith: I love to perform. That's why I do it. And I need to perform in order to sell CDs and make a living. Also I love the sense of "shared experience" that an evening of live music can afford. I always marvel that the more personal the work, the more universal it is. So I try to recall how I felt when I wrote the song and deliver it with that emotion.

Some nights you can literally feel your songs drawing an audience together as each person interprets the songs from their own paradigm. It's kind of surreal to spend an evening celebrating and lamenting life with a group of strangers who, by the last songs, no longer feel like strangers.

I enjoy playing other people's music for fun until eventually something of my own bubbles up; if not in words, at least a melodic idea for an instrumental piece that produces some kind of emotional response.

Mae Moore: I perform my own songs because the words are true for me. They are often "my story" and therefore resonate honestly with the audience. I was once in a position when I had a major label deal where they wanted me to record a song that lyrically, I couldn't get behind. It simply wasn't true for me and it felt awkward to sing the lyric. We had quite a showdown over that one and the label finally backed down.

Since we are all human and have gone through similar experiences, I find that people find meaning themselves in certain songs that are painted with a broad brush, that touch on common themes. Sometimes it can be just a single phrase that has meaning for them or sometimes it is a musical hook that they enjoy.

KJ Denhert: I have some passionate fans and sometimes I wonder how different the songs sound to them. I imagine we all have a style of listening to music and I can't know anybody else's truly. I think from comments that I hear that many people listen to lyrics a lot more closely than I do. I absolutely have to be drawn in by melody and chord progression before I'll listen to a lyric.

I have been a part of songwriters' circles or song contests where I am sure that I am getting the "German Shepherd look". By that I mean the way a dog will stop and tilt its head as though they can say "huh"?

I really don't like purists (jazz, folk and rock are filled with 'em). I experience more non- musician purists, than musician purists but they're out there. Purists are my arch rivals if I was a superhero – I'd fly the earth seeking to reform purists into centrists.

Lorraine Hart: I perform a lot of the songs I write because they mean something to me. I perform other people's songs because I have found meaning in them…and I speak about both lyrics and music while using the word, meaning. What I can't do is sing something that doesn't resonate for me. Example – Natural Woman – you think, cool song right? When you grow up in a household where women are supposed to behave themselves, are nothing without a man, these lyrics begin to feel a little like a chicken bone in the craw, the melody whining. I performed this song once and put it away. I'm not saying it isn't a brilliant song, just not for my repertoire. Example the opposite way – Sixteen Tons – ooo, the rhythm, the climb to that explosive last line…and who can't relate to owing their soul to the company store, male or female? It's a brilliant song because everyone knows their own measure of the sixteen tons and that melody rides you up the tram's rails.

The answer's been the same for nearly forty years; I write, sing and perform because I was an addict from the first "fix" and it saved my life…oh, happy servitude!

Jane Eamon: I have learned how to pay homage to writers I love. By singing their songs, I share their experiences when they wrote the songs. I translate it in my way and try to make it true for me.

Chapter 7

Finding your own voice

As in any art form, it is essential for an artist to find their own original and unique voice. As a songwriter, it's mandatory. You cannot copy other writers forever and be truthful to you (unless you are a tribute band). But in the beginning stages of learning how to write songs, you often start out playing like those you've been influenced by.

I liked a lot of people when I first started writing. I didn't know I had a voice that was uniquely my own. I never let it out. I had to go through the process of finding out who I really was.

I didn't like the sound of my own voice. I was timid about opening up when I sang. But my writing was beginning to be more than a copy of someone else's. I was learning how to fashion words in my own way and come up with something unique to me.

It's not always that simple. If you listen to popular music, you are bombarded with the sounds and shapes of what is current. You can't help but assimilate some of that into your own way of writing and playing. I've met a lot of young writers who use clichés and trite phrases in their songs because that's what they've heard. It's tough to convince them to look for different ways to say the same thing, like I love you, or my heart is broken.

But it's essential to becoming a good songwriter, to find the balance between unique and universal. It may look easy from the outside, but it's not.

There is a very fine line between good and bad. That's where the voice comes in, the writer's voice, the place where your own take on the world is valid and accepted by both you and an audience.

Jory Nash: Interesting…I remember learning how to play the guitar and trying to write songs like Neil Young. Same thing with the piano and Bruce Springsteen. At some point I stopped thinking about the other artists and just wrote. But without those shoulders to climb on I wouldn't have "found" my own.

Andrew Smith: Every great artist knows very well how much they owe to great artists who have come before them.

Jory Nash: Another thought: My songwriting particularly the lyrical content has changed from my first CD through my 5th. The songs I'm writing now I definitely wouldn't/couldn't have years ago. That doesn't make the new ones better or worse. Just different and reflective of where I am musically, lyrically, life-istically (there's a new word!), right now. So although I think I "found" my voice a long time ago, the timbre of that voice keeps changing on me. It would be really boring otherwise.

Jane Eamon: That is worthwhile noting that we do change our voices over time. Not just the singing voice but the way we write and look at the world. It can be affected by so many things and can't possibly stay in one place forever.

Kristin Sweetland: The very most important thing about writing is having something to say. There is nothing so powerful as a writer possessed of their own voice. It is what elevates good writing to great writing.

Maria Dunn: Sing! Unaccompanied! Don't listen too much to one artist all the time – keep your listening diverse so that you don't end up sounding like the latest imitation of Ani Difranco or Aretha Franklin (as admirable as both of these artists are) rather than yourself.

KJ Denhert: In two words "patience and faith".

Barry Mathers: It just came naturally after we quit being a cover band.

Shari Ulrich: To me singing and playing is honouring the power and beauty of the gift of music. If we engage in it as an external means to fill a hole of insecurity, it's harder to find one's voice, because it becomes a search to find affirmation. If you don't try so hard to get that and write and sing with utter honesty, you will find your own voice.

Lorraine Hart: (Think haunting bluegrass) So many ways…so many voices…so little tiiime….afore I go…..

I'll never forget the exploding excitement of the moment I let my singing voice go. In a high school hall at fourteen I rattled every locker, letting freedom ring…in my first enslaving fix. Nearly forty years later, it's been styled, sculpted, trained and organically grown into an instrument more intimate to me than any lover, each fix of letting go leaving me higher than the last. I feel new all over again as I learn to mix in the subtle smoky memories only age and experience bring.

Just as the physical voice goes on a lifetime journey, so does the writer's voice….perhaps more accurate to say, voices. You can see why there's madness involved. Musicians, storytellers…artists…have always been part of the Shamanic family of the tribe of Man. I see nods of agreement in the gallery. Who hasn't had a song suddenly become a most powerful portal within and without…we're talking down the rabbit hole and through the looking-glass…..with safe return. All hands raised!!!!

Jane Eamon: I think we colour our voices with our experiences. But as long as it's authentic and truthful, it works both inside and out. We can't quiet the voice, it speaks to us alone. We can choose to ignore it, but it will keep coming back more insistent each time. Eventually you give in to it, or you silence it forever and that's a tragedy. We don't always have to write in our own voices, but it seems like a waste of time not to. What better way is there to express our true selves then by using our true voices?

Ian Thomas: Ultimately the exercise might be striving for what feels the most honest. This is an ongoing pursuit.

Chapter 8

Eve Goldberg on Songwriting

I asked my friend, Eve Goldberg, to share her thoughts on songwriting. She in turn, did not answer the questions, she wrote this amazing essay and I thought it worthy of including as it was sent to me. It is used with permission.

"What is a song? On the surface, it is words sung to a melody. Simple enough. But songs are complex creatures that work or don't work on many levels. On a musical level, songs have melodic, harmonic, and rhythmic structures. They can follow or break musical conventions; they can be at different tempos, and in different time signatures. They can mix tempos and time signatures. A song can change key, or visit other keys and come back to the first key. A song can musically draw on or refer to other songs or styles. The music can be discordant, harmonious, energizing, melancholy, driving, simple, complex, funny, touching, sexy, inspiring, or relaxing.

The words can be from the point of view of an object, a person, a deity, or an animal. They can speak from first person, second person, or third person. They can be about nothing. They can be about everything. The lyrics can be playful, happy, sad, personal, technical, angry, old-fashioned, modern, spiritual, or thoroughly common.

The song can have rhymes. Or not. Techniques like onamatopoetry, alliteration, internal rhyme may or may not be used. The words might be concrete. Or they might be abstract. The meaning might be ambiguous, or it might be totally transparent. Metaphor and simile will certainly be there, but they can be more or less obvious, used in different ways, mixed, or not. The words can "match" the melody in tone or feel. Or they can be juxtaposed. The song form can be simple or complex. There can be an introduction, verses, refrains, choruses, bridges, tags, and codas. There can be a lot of repetition, or very little.

Songs can serve a higher purpose, or they can be just for fun. Or both. A song can evoke strong memories, be a powerful tool for change, make you cry, inspire you to shake your booty, or get you into bed with someone. Songs can reflect and express the hopes, desires, fears, and triumphs of a person, or of a whole community or culture. They can be created in situations of incredible adversity and oppression. They can be of the moment, or they can strike a chord that lasts centuries.

So how do we go about creating these miniature masterpieces that we call songs? I think the answer will be different for every songwriter, and in a way, one of the tasks of the songwriter is to figure out what works for them and go with it. What's right for me might not work at all for you, and vice versa. Discovering the tools and methods that help you create your best songs will be a lifelong journey if you choose to follow that path. So, herewith, a collection of ideas that have helped me so far along my path – take them or leave them as you choose.

I am a late bloomer in songwriting terms. I avoided writing songs for many years because I thought I had nothing to say that hadn't already been said. I grew up surrounded by a wealth of contemporary and traditional folk, blues, and country music, and I learned a healthy respect for songs and the people who make them. When I began performing, I sang a mixture of traditional songs and songs by other writers. I spent a lot of time getting inside those songs, and understanding them, in order to be able to sing them effectively. I didn't know it then, but those songs were my first lessons in songwriting, and I still return to them often. Learning and singing other people's songs, or traditional songs, is one of the best ways I know to understand what makes a song work.

One reason I didn't write songs for a long time was that I thought I had to write something deep and meaningful that bared my soul, changed the world, moved my audience to tears, had no relationship to anything that had ever come before, and would be worthy of being recorded by Bonnie Raitt or Emmylou Harris—a tall order for a budding songwriter. It was only when I left those impossible ideals behind that I began discovering my own way into writing.

My first song was a simple blues that I'm still pretty fond of. It doesn't have lots of words, it repeats a lot, and it doesn't say anything profound about the world, my life, or anything really. But I think it's a damn good song. In retrospect, I realize it was a clever way to start writing. I started with something I already knew – the blues form. By deciding I wanted to write a song in a particular style, I gave myself a frame to work within, a frame that had some rules I knew and understood. "A blues song" suggested chord structure, language, subject matter, verse form, and a bunch of other variables that I didn't have to wrestle with. Ironically, imposing a set of limitations was liberating. That first song taught me that originality is not about being completely new and different. What's original about that song is that I took familiar elements and put them together in a fresh way, with my own quirky spin. Writing that first song taught me that songs can be simple, and they can be meaningful even if you don't rip your heart out of your chest and plop it on the table in front of your audience.

Since then, I've tried my hand at writing songs in a bunch of different styles, and although it's not the only way I write songs anymore, I still use that technique because it works for me. I've even taken an existing song, re-written the words, and then re-written the melody and chord structure underneath. Most listeners would never connect the new song with the existing song it was based on. It's a great way to explore song forms, and while some people might turn up their nose, I say if it works, why not? (I just make sure that I've changed enough elements that the two songs are truly different from each other.)

As I started exploring different musical styles in my writing, I also realized that I do have things to say. Writing songs helped me recognize that I have a unique perspective on life, just like every other person has a unique perspective on life. My job as a songwriter is to speak from that unique perspective in a way that touches my audience. For me, that means getting as close as I can to the truth of what I'm thinking or feeling about something, and expressing that truth in a way that resonates with other people. My goal when I write a song, even if it's about something very personal, is for the listener to say, "yeah, that happened to me" or "I've been through something like that," or "I feel like that, too."

And let's face it, there are certain things all human beings go through: we're all born, we all grow and change, we fall in love (or lust), we fall out of love (or lust), we search for purpose and meaning, we work, we succeed and fail at things, we experience loss, we feel joy, we respond to events in the world around us, we get older, we die, and so on. Whatever the variations are, I can't think of any songs that don't relate to one or more of these basic human experiences. That's one of the reasons we love songs –they are meditations on things that we already know.

The audience part of it is important for me. If I were writing songs purely for myself, I wouldn't care how universal the themes were. My songs would be personally therapeutic, cathartic, far more specific, and probably pretty cryptic. And there's nothing wrong with using music in that way. But as soon as I take the step of singing a song to someone else, I'm taking on a certain responsibility. They are privileging me with their time and attention, and I need to earn and keep their trust by respecting that time and attention. So whatever I'm trying to say, wherever I want to take them, I need to say it in a way that my audience will want to follow me.

What I'm aiming for, when I write, is clarity. If people seem confused when I sing my song, I know I'm not done yet – I've got to go back and figure out what's not clear, what can be left out, and what can be simplified. Sometimes I think simplicity gets a bad rap, as if being simple somehow means you are sacrificing artistic value. But I think some of the most beautiful artistic statements are actually pretty simple. And it's not easy to say something in a simple way. Mississippi John Hurt, John Prine, David Francey, and Gillian Welch are all examples of musicians whose art is elegantly simple.

Mostly I'm not concerned with commercial success when I'm writing. I'm writing for myself and for my imagined audience. Of course I hope people will like the songs enough to buy my CD or pay to hear me perform them, but I try not to let that be my incentive for writing. It gets back to that idea of speaking the truth about the things I think and feel about the world. If making money were my only focus, I would have a hard time holding on to the core of why I write. Fortunately, as a folk/roots artist, I have the luxury of existing in a realm a little bit outside the mainstream music industry – a realm where success is measured in kinder terms, for the most part.

Having said that, I have great respect for writers who are able to make a living in the commercial music world.

The Songwriter's Voice

There's a lot to be learned from songs aimed for a commercial market, and there are many examples of very fine songs that have achieved commercial success. And there are also examples of writers who did not start out writing for the commercial music industry, whose songs were later picked up and became wildly popular. So it can happen in many different ways.

One of the key things for me is to keep a sense of balance in my life. I don't rely on songwriting alone for my income. I am a performer, a recording artist, a teacher, AND a songwriter. And between all those things, I seem to be able to scrape together enough money to make me happy, more or less, most of the time. I think it was Utah Phillips who said something to the effect that "you can make a living from folk music. Not a killing, but a living." And that's my aim as a folk/roots musician and a songwriter. Of course, like any songwriter, I have utopian fantasies about my songs being recorded by my musical heroes and selling millions of copies. And if that happened to me, well, I guess I would just cash the cheques and say "thank you".

All of us will go through self-doubt and questioning at some point. And we all have times in our lives when we aren't able to follow our creative impulses – maybe we're working too hard, or we have to juggle family responsibilities, or we are struggling with life in some way. Everyone is going to have a different path, and the path you are on is part of what makes you who you are. Perhaps you are not where you want to be, but what you are experiencing is shaping your sensibility and your response to the world, and that will become part of whatever creative endeavors you might pursue. When I haven't been able to pursue my bliss, I've tried to take solace in the tiny moments of inspiration and creativity that I can squeeze into my life. Sometimes I would hum to myself while I worked, or walked. Sometimes I would take five minutes to play my guitar or write something down before I went to bed.

I used to be afraid that if I didn't stop and work on the song idea I was having at that very moment, it would completely disappear. I recently read Natalie Goldberg's excellent book "Writing Down the Bones," and it gave me some reassurance about that fear. Goldberg talks about "the composter," which is like a subconscious creative cauldron inside us. All our life experiences go into the cauldron and mix together and interact to make our creative "compost". If we are able to take the time to listen, creative ideas will inevitably bubble up from the "composter". If we aren't able to record or work on those ideas, it's true we might not be able to fully reproduce them later, but whatever we were thinking will sink back into the cauldron, and if it's a really good idea, it's going to bubble up in some other way at some other time. So nothing is truly lost. Thinking about my creative process that way has really helped me lighten up about my songwriting ideas.

And it is very easy to get down on yourself about your own creative process. We all have those voices inside our heads that tell us we're not good enough, we should just give up, and what makes us think we can write songs anyway? Over time, I've come to recognize these voices as part of me, and develop some strategies to work with them.

One way that I work with them is that I don't try to sit and write for long periods of time. My process is very piecemeal. I might jot down an idea one day, come back to it another day and play around with it, come back to it again in a few weeks, and so on. I find if I keep the beginning of the process exploratory and playful, and don't put the pressure on to create a finished song, I'm able to generate much more material. But ultimately, I usually need to buckle down at some point and force myself to fashion some kind of finished song out of all my explorations. Deadlines can be good things! I've started to think that the songwriting process involves two different characters with very different needs and ideas. I call them "the creator" and "the editor".

The creator thrives on play, brainstorming, impulse, improvisation, expression, emotion, etc. and is the source of the material. The creator is a lateral thinker, doesn't care if things make sense, and is good at making connections. The creator is concerned with internal thoughts, feelings, and beliefs. The creator can get overly attached to his/her creations.

The editor is about polishing and crafting the material, and is concerned with grammar, syntax, continuity, structure, believability, true rhyme, subtlety, problem-solving, making things perfect. The editor has a good eye for detail and is focused on the listener. The editor can be quite critical. They each need to have their turn, but it's important to let the creator generate the material before the editor steps in. If the editor comes in too soon, the creator will shut down and you won't have the material to work with. If the creator is allowed to work without any limits, what you create will suffer from not being polished or crafted. They each need their time and space, so I find it's important to identify for myself whether I'm in the creating stage or the editing stage, and to try to hand over the songwriting platform to the appropriate character.

For me, writing songs has been all about pushing myself. When I started writing songs, it was a big leap for me to sing a song in public and say that I had written it (in fact, the first time I sang my own song in public I didn't tell anyone it was my song). As I have grown as a songwriter, there is always a new edge to push at. Sometimes it's about writing something that's deeply personal. Sometimes it's writing in a different style or genre. Sometimes it's writing about a political situation. Sometimes it's about writing a song from a place of anger. Sometimes it's writing a funny song. Whatever that edge is, I have found that if I take myself to that edge and explore it honestly, I am able to create songs that reward me ten thousand times over, whether or not anyone else thinks they are any good.

You'll notice I used the word "honestly" when I talked about exploring my edges. That's a critical element. Songs can be just as shallow and dishonest, or just as profound and meaningful as any other form of human expression—or anything in between. The payoff for me has come when I have forced myself to go beyond platitudes and formulas and into those uncharted waters where I'm not exactly sure what I'm doing.

So there you have it. There are a thousand other things I could have talked about, but those are the bits and pieces I have to offer you today. Songwriting is just one of our tools as musicians and as human beings on this earth, a way of making sense of this bizarre, kaleidoscopic, and wondrous world we live in. No matter what structure they follow; what style they are in, what they are about; whether the words rhyme or not; whether they make you laugh, cry, or both, songs are like tiny miracles. They nourish and sustain us, bring us to a better place, help us celebrate and remember. Songs can take us to the hidden parts of our own souls, they can lift us up and help us stand, and they are there through the triumphs and tragedies of our lives.

Ultimately, songs affirm that we are not alone.

Chapter 9

Do we always have to be hopeful? What about songs of outrage and anger? Of God? Are some subjects taboo?

In the early stages of my songwriting career, I was writing a lot about how I felt. Usually it was angst over whatever passed for drama in my young life. I found these songs the easiest to write as I was in the depths of emotional turmoil. I believe it provided a lot of material for this budding songwriter, to be able to pour out my anguish in song. But I was beginning to think that maybe it was more important to uplift my listeners, to make them happy. Or write songs about subjects not so easily accepted, like serial killers and God.

I did write a song called, "Show Me" about the existence of God. It was full of anger and outrage that God had allowed terrible things to happen in the world and seemingly watched from afar. I don't know if the song was any good, but I thought it was important to talk about it.

It made me think that perhaps there were things better left unsaid, things that folks didn't really want to think about. But like waving a red flag in front of a bull, I wanted to write about them. I wrote a song called "Aunt Kitty" about Alzheimer's disease. I remember Bill Henderson, in a workshop, telling me I shouldn't be writing about that because it was too close to home to aging baby boomers. But I wrote it anyway and I'm glad I did. It's a good song.

I did wonder though, if my audiences were turned off by the subject matter of some of my songs. I wondered if I should be writing more upbeat, happy songs instead. Were there subjects better left untouched?

Maria Dunn: It helps not to decimate your listeners'/audience's hopes! It can be good for a writer to just tell it like it is sometimes – sing a sad song or a murder ballad. It's all in the balance. If you are going to do one song that is bleak, you need to offer listeners one that isn't.

A good song is less about you, the songwriter, experiencing the emotion and more about how the listener experiences it. If it is a subject or story that deserves outrage or an expression of anger, think of how you can get that across most effectively and don't sacrifice the music to the emotion. Otherwise, you've just written a bad song and no one is going to listen to it anyway. Or they'll be turned off the subject or story because of your bad song!

And if you are too emotional yourself when you perform it, you probably won't perform it as well as you would like to. The best time to really allow yourself that outpouring of grief or anger or outrage is while you're **writing** the song. By the time you've worked it up to performance; you should have taken an emotional step backwards so that you can perform it well. Then, if it's a good song, the listener will feel the emotion that you initially felt and that you wanted them to feel.

David Essig: For me, there always has to be hope and compassion. These are the liberating qualities of art – the things that we are blessed at being able to do. I like to think that the artist has not only the ability but the responsibility to (and I'm paraphrasing Jurgen Habermas here) "emancipate us from the imprisoning horizon of the immediate."

Shari Ulrich: I tend to be hopeful, but there are lots of writers who just like to plumb the depths of the darkness and it serves a purpose for the listener too. Songs of outrage and anger can allow people to "feel" their outrage and anger, which serve a valuable purpose too. I'm an optimist, so it's my nature to want to bring hope into all my songs.

Barry Mathers: I don't think we always have to be hopeful, but if the lyrics are kind of a downer I try and use an up-tempo or pretty melody to help them along.

Andrew Smith: I, like most people, enjoy hopeful songs too, but I think some of the very best songs are raw laments that convince you that there is NO light at the end of the tunnel. Simply by expressing a song of despair, a songwriter can actually share the burden of a hopeless heart, a heart that just needs to hear that someone else has felt this low. Thus, the most hopeless songs can carry the seeds of new hope.

I think an artist strives to be more than a good entertainer, more than a good craftsman. And so the artist won't shy away from difficult and messy questions and issues.

Norm Strauss: Sometimes I think my job as a writer is just to articulate the journey, not necessarily pretend to know the outcome of every trial. I am naturally a fairly "hopeful" person so my music usually tends to go there. But sometimes I have heard songs that don't contain a shred of hope in them and yet they are beautiful and uplifting. Some of the Psalms of the Bible are like that. They articulate the mystery but offer no solution. That causes us to dig the well for ourselves instead of always looking for a hand-out.

Some writers have recognized that anger is a very powerful emotion and because they want to write powerfully emotive songs they use it like a tool to gain an audience. I find that quite unimaginative and slightly annoying. In fact, I think I would like to write a protest song about that!

Jory Nash: There is no God. I don't need to question it. Probably half my songs have explored my denial of God. But conversely I do believe in the power of faith and am somewhat jealous of those who blithely believe. And then too, the Bibles have wonderful stories that make good song fodder.

Barry Mathers: I wrote a song called "Don't Drink the Water" about a lead smelter that polluted the Columbia River for years and it's a pretty angry song but one of my favourites. Some subjects are taboo as far as radio goes. I wrote with a Nashville writer recently who had a song about child molestation and was told time after time by music publishers that no one would ever touch it because of its subject nature.

Andrew Smith: I certainly don't think negative emotions and hard questions are taboo for a songwriter. However, it is true that some songs are offensive and it can be in bad taste (and not in the performer's best interests) to perform them in *some situations*. For example, I sang a funny song about road rage one night and half the audience got up and left. I learned later that a teenager in town had died in a similar way described in the song, (very bad taste and timing). I was performing in the US a song of mine called "Democracy for Money" shortly after the US went to war with Iraq. The room was full of patriotic republicans and the atmosphere went very cold for the rest of the evening. I may still have played the tune had I known this – but I'd have left it until near the end of the night....

Yael Wand: Some subjects are taboo for me as a writer. Usually these have to do with my relationships to those I love – I think it can be unfair of me to share the details of a relationship in a song without permission of my friend or family member. They didn't ask to be written about. Still, this is a challenge for me to write about a certain topic in a less direct and possibly more creative fashion.

Personally, I have difficultly writing about overtly political topics. I can't shake the preachy-ness of stating my political beliefs. Yet I feel that as a whole my writing screams out my political views about the world and our relationship to it and to one another.

David Essig: I tend to think of this as a craft issue. Once you've taken on the responsibility to write about something difficult, you need to find a way to do it that doesn't barrage and pummel the listener. You need to find that oblique angle and come at if from the side. Slamming right into the middle of an issue never works well for me – it's the old adage of "show, don't tell."

Ian Thomas: Some writers of course can take any subject, taboo or seedy and make it palatable. Such, is the beauty of metaphor and melody in the hands of a skilled writer. It's a bit like that old expression; some people can get away with swearing when others just sound disgusting. The direct answer to the question is that too much hope, too much anger, or too much religion can make for an insipid or depressing listening experience. Many of the most successful songs straddle the sweet-sadness of life without crossing the line and hold a little room for the listener to breathe.

Kristin Sweetland: Definitely the hopeful is not necessary...great songs can still be great even if they are entirely miserable. Although sometimes being miserable from a song can thoroughly uplift the senses...can it not?

Are songs of outrage and anger less effective when the audience is bombarded with negative emotions? Not less effective, but possibly effective in different ways. And yes please to the questioning nature of God. I believe these subjects are as critical to writers as they always have been throughout history. Taboo is subjective. I think being aware of where you perform songs of a certain nature is wise though....but I will always and forever endlessly advocate standing up for what you truly believe in through your art. REVOLUTION!

KJ Denhert: For my sound I do try to balance hope with realistic lyrics. The truth slips out anyway. Some things are taboo for me and some words too. If you are a singer/ songwriter and you want to perform your own songs as I do, I need to be able to perform them authentically. I welcome writing for other people especially if they can define who the singer they want to represent is. That becomes craft at its best and is liberating.

I think a song can be written questioning God's existence and think there are millions out there that already do. The musical, "The Book of Mormon" on Broadway broke a lot of rules of propriety and is a huge hit for doing just that!

Hal Brolund: Some stories are hopeful, some are dark, some are uplifting, some are simply narrative. I think commercial music is obsessed with the "happy ending". Lately though, there are some dark songs making their way in the world. If the function of the storyteller is to tell stories that resonate with the audience, perhaps it is a function of the times we live in whether they are needed to soothe or not.

A subject is only taboo if the artist finds it so. That doesn't mean that the audience will accept any statement the artist wants to make. So questioning the existence of God is fine but take care to also question the existence of the Devil.

Barry Mathers: Don Schlitz, who wrote "The Gambler", told me that there are only five subjects to write about, falling in love, falling out of love, being in love, wishing you were in love and wishing you weren't in love. The point he was trying to make is that you need to write songs that people can relate to.

Norm Strauss: I can't imagine God being insecure about you questioning His existence so personally I'm not either. If you read some of the songwriters in the Old Testament, you'll see that they wrote songs all over the emotional spectrum including lots of "where are you, God?" songs. I think that can be very healthy. Are you outraged? Sure, write a song about it, but don't get upset if people don't agree with why you are outraged. If you can deal with that reaction, then by all means write that flip the world a bird song. Less effective because it's negative? No, sometimes a good protest song does the world some good. Just be ready to handle the feedback, that's all and don't expect me to agree with your protest song, just because it's clever or passionate. Some subjects taboo? If you are an abusive, self-loathing, foul-mouthed person, and your songs reflect that about you, don't expect me to play your songs in my house. I have children whom I'm trying to teach to be respectful people. Thank you very much.

Mae Moore: Be true to yourself. Otherwise you will wind up sounding insincere, a trait that people easily pick up on and are put off by.

Jane Eamon: The truth of something is often the most painful part. But by speaking truth, we unlock something inside of us and by doing so, hopefully can do the same for others. That's why I think it's almost mandatory for a writer to write about whatever disturbs him or herself the most.

Jory Nash: This songwriter doesn't feel he HAS to be ANYTHING (hopeful or otherwise). I just am. Perhaps that's too existential or nihilistic. I don't know. But someone can get the same feeling of soul-soothing by having a song depress them as another person can by having a different song uplift them. My role, or job, is to write the best I can, to try to get down in the song what I hear in my head. C'est tout. The word "hope" or concept thereof never enters into my mind when I write a song, except to say I "hope" I can keep writing interesting songs.

When I think about it a little more most of my favourite writers employ melancholy or sadness more than hope in their lyrics. Musically, I think it's harder to define emotions thus so. Upbeat does not always equal happy; slow and mellow does not necessarily equal sad or lazy.

Any and all emotions are fair game for the writer. What they feel when writing is not necessarily what the listener will pick up on or get themselves.

Mae Moore: I recall when rap music was first being heard on the radio with their strong and impactful lyrics. A lot of those lyrics were directed at white society's abusive and hypocritical treatment of African Americans. Some were shocking and hard to take....but afforded us a very real insight into how some people were feeling, that we might not otherwise have experienced. Personally, I think freedom of expression is needed as long as it doesn't promote hatred and killing. Folk music has been the historical champion of the rights of the individual.

Lorraine Hart: Of course we don't have to always be hopeful. In fact, if we were only that, I'm sure audiences would come after us with big sticks at some point for being so bloody annoying! It's in the nature of music to be what's required. Look at the Blues, angry chaotic Rock, rousing anthems of change that move millions in the way they need to be moved. It is the power of the woven music and lyrics to speak to whatever emotions...first the emotion of the writer and then of the listener.....that is the point.

If you live in a country of free speech, there are no taboo subjects. That having been said, a writer is responsible for their words and better be prepared to meet an equal and opposite reaction from a listener who feels violated. You better know what you meant to say because it's guarandamnteed someone will read it entirely differently. Randy Newman wrote a brilliant song about prejudice and was immediately accused of being.....you guessed it.....prejudiced!

What about songs of outrage and anger? Lady Day's "Strange Fruit" leaps to mind and I'm gripped in its powerful effect immediately. We have a need and they (the songs of outrage and anger) tap the pain that would kill us were it not expressed. It's more a release from the bombardment and incredibly effective.

Question anything you want to question. Hopefully you know the difference between searching for answers, cutting edge...and bad taste sensationalism. You're on your own.

Jane Eamon: It's the questioning that's important not so much the writing. We have to question things, it's how we learn. We can't learn if we accept everything we read, see, hear, whatever. As an intelligent human being, it's my job and duty to ask why something is the way it is. Even if there's no easy answer, I can still ask and perhaps come to an understanding of why I can't understand something.

Jory Nash: Yes, some subjects are taboo. Any subject that a writer cannot write about in an interesting way should be taboo. Which is to say that all subjects are taboo and no subjects are taboo. Only subjects where the writer is talking jive or writing badly about are taboo in my opinion.

I could say that writing about serial killers and their explicit actions would be taboo. Tough subject that no one really would want to hear about. But then Sufjan Stevens recently went and wrote a chilling narrative portrait of John Wayne Gacy that is clever, explicit and honest. It's a subject that I couldn't have touched, but Stevens could and he did it well. It was taboo to me only because I couldn't write it if I tried. For him it was an inspiration. It probably has as many detractors as acolytes.

Can you be a good songwriter without asking tough questions? Do we always have to be entertainers?

Lynn Harrison: It seems to me the toughest questions and the most important and essential for any people (songwriters or not) are the ones that seek to clarify the meaning of one's life. Questions such as: Who am I? What do I value? What was that about? Am I telling the truth or deceiving myself (or others)? What is beautiful? How can I serve others? Is this the best I can do? To the extent that we are conscious of these questions and seek to answer them, we mature as individuals. Apply these questions to any task and you're likely to get better at it. In the course of the songwriting process, those "questions" are framed as creative choices which are often "lightening-fast" (Do I like that chord? Is that the most precise word available? Does this note make sense?), but they are all "tough questions" in that they come down to "what matters?" and "how can I serve that which matters?" In other words, you write songs that have integrity in the same way you try to live with integrity: one choice at a time, maturing along the way with a sense of responsibility toward yourself and others. That's how I see it anyway.

David Essig: Have courage to say the difficult things, to write the song no one wants to hear, to tell the story that is not comfortable.

Shari Ulrich: I never think about the element of asking questions when I write. I think the courage is in the creativity – which does not always include asking questions. Sometimes the courage is in writing about aspects of being human that people generally hold onto as a secret. I like to bring the secrets into the daylight.

David Essig: Entertainers are good – it's just another line of work from what I do. I think of myself as a poetic storyteller with a guitar and some stories to tell. If the listeners find this entertaining, all the better. Courage is the key.

KJ Denhert: There is nothing nobler than a truly gifted entertainer. An entertainer can change the way you feel by example not by preaching or explaining but by connecting to what they are doing. I think you may be referring to the performer for whom a gig is only a paycheque. We all try to avoid that but have probably had to go through the motion once or twice. Yes I hate that.

David Borins: This is an "art for art's sake" vs. "art as an agent for a higher purpose" debate. If you aren't willing to ask tough questions, you can still be a great songwriter, but I'd avoid choosing journalism or politics as a vocation.

Chapter 10

Do you believe in channelling the Muse? Has it ever astounded you to see and hear something you've written? Some have called it Divine, others God, others a spiritual gift...what are your views? Do you think about this?

What is the Muse? The dictionary definition is that in ancient Greek mythology, she is one of 9 daughters of Zeus and Mnemosyne; a protector of an art or science. The Muse is also the source of an artist's inspiration, the idea, germ, the creative seed. But where does it come from? Ah, there's the question. Nobody knows. Without sounding too terribly cosmic, it is at best, I think, an illusive connection to spirit. It cannot be called at will, doesn't always listen to you, has no respect for timing, can be triggered by the strangest things, will sometimes take you to places you least expect and is not always clear. It will follow you around for days repeating a line over and over in your head enough to drive you mad. And then it will disappear for months at a time.

There is no point in arguing with the Muse. It does not care. If you are a writer of pretty love songs in the key of G, the Muse may show you a hard-edge pop song in the key of A flat. You have to listen. It will lead you down strange pathways often with interesting results.

Many times I've had the perfect line show up in the middle of the night and have not gotten up to write it down. Morning comes, and you guessed it – I can't remember it. It happens a lot.

My first experience with a channeled song was "The Soldier's Lament". The lines....

Lord I've been thinking here in the mud
That lately you've gone away
I'm tired, stinkin', smelling of blood
And I don't have the strength to pray

....showed up. I had no idea what the song was about. I did find out later it was a story of a young man who died in the Civil War. How could I have known that? I didn't question it, I just wrote it. But it was more than a little creepy. So yes, I believe in the Muse. I believe in channelling. I believe we are contacted when there is something to say and maybe we are the vessel who can get the story out.

Shari Ulrich: Channelling the Muse, that's the only way I can describe the magic when it happens. I feel like it comes "through" me – and I take credit for putting myself in the place where it can happen, and for the work of finishing it to have life as a song, but the spark...that's something "other".

KJ Denhert: I like to think that what I am meant to do comes easily to me. What I am not meant to do is harder. But that hasn't always held up when tested. It takes so much confidence to keep pushing, trying, recording, spending, investing and booking gigs. It can become an ego-danger zone if I am not mindful.

Kristin Sweetland: I absolutely believe in the Muse. I call to her often like Dante in Purgatorio: "Let the dead poetry rise again, O sacred Muse for I am yours and here let Calliope arise." I also believe in hard work and the CRAFT of writing. I've had Muse moments and pure moments of scientific rationalist songwriting. I think learning to balance the two is the key to great songwriting.

"Crafting" songs is the ultimate rush! There is nothing like the high that comes with that "eureka" moment when you tie everything together...mmmm, victory. The number one thing I think of is the artistic merit of the song and the pure level of craftsmanship. I also try not to be too abstract so much that my intended audience won't be able to understand what I'm saying. I have learned that cryptic is only so good...poetry is better.

Ed Winacott: Earlier in my life, I sometimes worried that whatever was causing me to write songs would suddenly disappear and be gone forever. This was especially so when I experienced long periods of nothing happening lyrically. This made me somewhat anxious – sort of felt a bit like an old testament type must have when the spirit had abandoned him. I'm more sanguine now and realize trying to make it happen doesn't work...I just have to have faith in ????? and it will work out again...just let it alone to be whatever it is.

How do I know when I'm called to write something? Well, when I'm caught up in the moment of the creation my mind is taken up with that and doesn't seem to have the ability to step back and say, "Hey I'm being called to write something." It's only afterward looking back that I become aware of the nature of the creation.

Where do the ones that write themselves come from? I'm not sure. Do we pick up on emotions from others and channel them or is it some of our own hidden emotions that have sneaked up on us? A lot of them start for me when my mind is otherwise engaged...looking elsewhere.

Whatever it is, I often find there is a lesson in there somewhere for me...but then that's probably the universal aspect of all human nature.

The Songwriter's Voice

Mae Moore: I wrote the song "Bohemia" or rather channeled the song in 15 minutes one afternoon after returning to Victoria from a writing sojourn in Australia. I was spellbound and felt my body tingling. It was an experience like no other. The lyric flowed through my pencil and onto the paper right before my eyes. We are conduits of a larger presence.

Andrew Smith: I believe in divine inspiration. Sometimes a work you've created, though it has come out of your very own brain and fingers, seems to exist and have its own life outside of you. It calls and speaks to you – the writer – as clearly as it does to anyone else. And it doesn't sound like your voice or your ideas. It's fascinating. And a bit creepy......

Ian Thomas: Most songwriters I know have experienced songs that have more or less written themselves. In these cases the songwriter is more conduit than craftsman. I do believe there is a spiritual evidence of a sort in the writing of some music or creation of art. I am not sure what God is so I can't chalk it up to him/her/it/them. I can say it is humbling to think that on occasion one doesn't have much to do with the writing of one's music.

Norm Strauss: Personally I don't believe in the concept of an impersonal force called a Muse that I am a servant to. To me, it's more about chiseling away at the rock to find out what is already hidden there. Sometimes the rock is hard and sometimes it's easy. I do believe in something called inspiration which comes from outside of me, but I believe the place that it comes from is not impersonal and has a vested interest in me as a whole person and not just as a songwriter. When I feel inspired I can write songs or give advice to a friend (or both at once).

Of course it's satisfying to write a great song because it affects people positively but success to me is not about songwriting only. It can be part of success but I tend to measure it by other, bigger things such as my family, relationships, longevity, mentoring and good laughs with old friends.

David Essig: I don't know about channelling the Muse, but I do know that I can barely remember the process of having written some of my most successful pieces. For me, it's all about keeping yourself open to the human condition and calling it like you see it.

Lorraine Hart: I believe the Muse comes to make love with the craftsman. Sometimes She is the completely dominant lover and I only follow Her lead. Sometimes I will begin the foreplay (sorry, being a Scorpio, this is my easiest metaphor!) but if I can't turn her on, it's a quick, masturbatory exercise (one could call that a pop tart song!) and neither of us is satisfied. When both of us are hungry for each other, it channels the behemoth void to create universes in.

I do believe the Muse channels others' stories and whispers in our ears...and yes, I've been astounded at the experience. Songwriters say all the time that our best songs seen to just write themselves. That having been said, I still feel it's important to bring the craftsman to the party and not abdicate for the purity of the received word...for, if that were the case, the Muse would play hanky-panky with everyone. Stories come to the storytellers; the sound emotions make, come to the musicians...and both come to the songwriter....for the purpose of crafting and re-telling the new.

The Songwriter's Voice

It has always been the Divine for me...the Muse being, after all, a goddess. When I was younger, there was an urgency to ask questions and try to define just what it all was. With age comes the wisdom to not "know" the answers so much...and understand more the questions within the context of the Great Mystery, textured with patterns and currents to flow with.

I go back to talking of the Shamanic experience within songs. You can travel in time on the "Good Ship Lollipop" to the thought of innocent moppets. You can travel to the tremendous sad-relief of the end of WWII on "We'll Meet Again", "Sentimental Journey" and such. Think of sacred music, whether coming from a cathedral, mosque, temple, sweat lodge, circle of stones, grove of trees, or hillside. We are co-creating when we're writing songs....how can we not see Creation's dance?

I think it's a lifetime search for we human beings to find both ourselves...and something greater than ourselves. In our need to listen, sing, play and write songs, is the first "something greater than ourselves", to be found. Floating with the dust in the footlights, between performer and audience, is the second. Everything we find beyond that, our own personal journey...both inward and outward.

Jory Nash: Don't know anything about Muses and Gods. But I do recognize when I'm more or less focused on writing and pretty much know if something good is going to come out during a particular session right from the start. Songwriting for me is work and talent combined and like any talent it needs practice to not get rusty.

Barry Mathers: It certainly helps to have the antennae up, meaning sitting down with a guitar and working at it. Then there are other times when the Muse appears and you need to stop whatever you are doing and write. This happens quite often to me just as I am about to fall asleep, or driving my bike. Any time the subconscious can take over is a good time for writing.

Ed Winacott: A fair number of the songs that I have written start while my mind is otherwise occupied…like when I'm driving or training in my boat or on skis (I know, I know, both coaches and driving instructors would say I should keep my mind on what I'm doing.)

The subject of the songs will often be some person or event that has moved me, but on occasion, I don't really know what it's about until some time after it's completed….at which point, I may discover that it really has been a message from one side of my brain to the other…something I should have known but was missing somehow. My songs are a way for me to try to touch some vague internal aspect of human nature…..mine or someone else's…the emotive, instinctual part rather than the rational part. The songs that I have written that have the most impact on me are often ones over which I feel I have exhibited very little control either in their inception or completion. I can neither make them start nor stop.

Maria Dunn: I've learned to keep my songwriting antennae up for good stories, turns of phrase all the time. If I get the hairs standing on the back of my neck, then I know my antennae have picked up something good, something worth trying to build into a song.

I have been humbled by some of my songs and hearing them used or sung by other people, or sung back to me from an audience. This has made me feel utterly grateful that I was able to write them and share them with people.

Norm Strauss: I don't think of it as channelling anything really. If I was able to do that I would like to channel Stevie Ray Vaughn and get some serious tones and also some fashion tips. But seriously, I think I prefer to think of it more as a secret whispered in my ear that I have been commissioned to develop and articulate. And if I don't do it, someone else probably will. Personally, yes I think this originates from God and is wrapped up in a whole lot of mystery that I have given up trying to figure it out. Generally though, I don't get too mystical about it. I know most writers would just think of it as an idea that "occurred" to them and they ran with it. But I cannot escape the feeling that many times I am being helped in the process. I need to be attentive during those times.

Bruce Madole: I was born to tell stories, I think and I have always written in a variety of forms – poetry first, then fiction and eventually lyrics. But underlying the variations in the actual form of the storytelling, there has almost always been a moment when an attention to the silence and my own thoughts led to a feeling of "emergence" like surfing on a wave of energy that sought to become a voice, or a form, or even just a single phrase that demanded in some way to be born on the page in my mind into song. Then all I needed to do was focus, to work and rework and to "attend" to the demands of literary and musical craft to see what this idea might become.

Jim Moffatt: I ask myself this question every time, "Is this just my ego?" It has to be true that there is some ego there but it goes way beyond that. The simplest is, "I write, therefore I am."

I actually hear myself thinking in song. Anything from the mundane to the serious but in my mind's "ear", I hear a melody and music when I'm pondering a problem or situation. Does that make me nuts? Maybe. But I don't write every song I "produce", only the ones that seem to make sense to share.

Why I do this is, it makes me a songwriter. In my live shows, I now have 3 songs that have a set melody and style but no written words. They are written on the spot as performed. My side man says it's his favourite parts of the show, to me, the scariest. I either soar or painfully crash and I have to be very careful about saying something stupid in the moment. But these moments result in the biggest connection, the deepest vibe and magic. It's for these moments that I write songs.

Norm Strauss: As far as "the muse" is concerned, I have never thought of creativity involving some kind of force that leaves me no choice but to write when the ideas start flowing. Personally, I have said "not today" many times even when ideas are flowing (to my own detriment of course). The reason? Usually because I am tired, or frustrated, or worst of all, when I listen to the voice in my head that says, "The world has enough great songs. Go have a nap." Anyway, I always have a choice whether to write or not. That is way scarier than not having a choice because you can develop a habit of not acting on what you are hearing and thereby dull your senses as a writer and as a person.

Joanne Stacey: The Muse is definitely part of my writing and I have written many songs while holding onto her tail as she is flying by. As well, there are some songs that I have written that have come directly "through" me and not "from" me. One in particular, "Lonesome Rambler" is a story about a guy who lived his life riding trains and trying to find his way. I have no connection to this type of story and feel that the owner of this story used me to tell it for him. This was more of a channelling, rather than the Muse, but either way, when you are open to receiving the message, it will come one way or another. I find that the Muse often visits when my mind is bored doing mundane things, like washing the dishes or taking a shower. Water seems to be a conduit for me.

How are you different for letting yourself be a servant to the Muse? How has it affected your life...your understanding of both life and self?

I must admit that the Muse scares me just a little. I've had more than one experience where songs have appeared that I know nothing about, subjects, names, dates, places, I couldn't possibly have known.

I've had tunes show up with chord diagrams in my head waiting for me to play them. I have learned to accept whatever comes and I try not to filter out what I can't understand. It's been a learning process and it's never predictable. I don't know from one day to the next, when I will be called.

I think that every writer has to come to terms with this at some point. They can choose not to accept its existence or just let it flow through and to them without trying to figure it out. It's like a current that gets turned on. It's exciting but also strange and mysterious.

Sometimes I just listen. Sometimes it is not clear what I'm supposed to do. Sometimes it fades in and out like a radio signal. Sometimes it says things I don't get. Does that make me crazy? No, but it does raise some serious questions about where it comes from.

Like I've said before, maybe I'm not supposed to know. I do know that it has opened my eyes to the underbelly of the waking world and made me a lot more receptive to things I don't understand. And that's a good thing.

Bruce Madole: It's kind of difficult for me to say how taking this path has changed me, if it has – but I decided at a fairly young age (around Grade 4) that I intended to be a writer "when I grow up", which I may do one day yet. So I have grown up with the understanding that there was a kind of magic you could plug into in various ways.

Ed Winacott: I stay open to the concept of being drawn along and don't fight it. How has it affected my life? It makes clear new insights of both me and the outside world and once these are known hopefully will inform my emotions and behaviour...in which case the outer journey is really just an extension of the inner.

The balance of control and receptivity? I often feel out of control once I let myself slide into the process and even the words "let myself" aren't all that accurate. Often I find the starting point occurs when I feel least in control of that portion of my brain....too tired or otherwise distracted to put up any roadblocks.

Here's one of the best. The other day I did a concert for elderly people and sang a song about my mother connecting with a friend that she hadn't seen in a long time. I was very unpresuming and almost reluctant to do so. The song is really about making every moment count, because time is finite for us all....my Mom was 85 at the time, all we can count on is the moment we are in.

Afterward an elderly lady came up and told me that song had reminded her of a very good friend with whom she had lost contact and that she made up her mind to make whatever effort was necessary to reconnect....that's success....a song going from the personal to the universal and somebody "getting it".

Ian Thomas: Songwriting might well be as much of an affliction as it is a talent or gift. It can often prevent one from living in the moment, as that moment is reduced to background noise by an idea in progress. Creativity is a constant distraction.

Now, strap creativity to the wheels of commerce and watch distraction turn to neurotic insecurity. Songwriting does help me understand life sometimes as I often have little revelations through it that move my consciousness forward ... albeit incrementally.

Chapter 11

Have you ever walked away from your songwriting, turned your back on the Muse?

In my early 20's, I pawned my guitar for $25 and went to sleep for 26+ years. I didn't play, write, sing or have anything to do with music in all that time. I abandoned my Muse.

It was like a big hole in me that I didn't know was there. I was filled with the Novocain of my own choosing. I became a non-musician. Folks who knew me during that time are now so amazed that I can sing and play. I was a different person.

I hear variations of this same story over and over again. People tell me of the numbing sleep and how wonderful it was to wake up. The reasons for waking are as unique as we all are but it's enough that we come back to our Muse.

I woke up in 1998. My husband dared me to write a song. It was for a contest and an opportunity to attend the BC Festival of the Arts with Stephen Fearing teaching songwriting. I wrote "Run to You", an instantly forgettable song. But it got me a spot in the class. I remember thinking they had made a mistake. I was the second oldest person there – at 46, already an old lady in my eyes in amongst the 20 somethings bright-eyed and record deal-laden. That week in Victoria changed my life. It showed me the possibility of being a songwriter. For the first time in a very long time, I felt alive and vibrating. I felt like I could do this. I felt connected. I was with people who thought the same way I did and it was an incredible feeling.

I went home and sold my house, quit my job and moved to

Victoria to seek my fame and fortune. I knew no one; I didn't have a place to live, a job or a support network. I spent the next six weeks in a B & B not playing or singing, but learning to live with myself by myself. It was horrible and scary and wonderful all at the same time. I was totally alone and responsible for no one but myself.

My soon-to-be husband came and proposed to me after three months apart and I came back to the Okanagan Valley. I vowed upon my return that I would devote as much of my life as I could to being a songwriter and I've never looked back.

I'd been given a second chance.

I don't know why I didn't play, write or sing for all those years. I've thought about that a lot. I really did feel like I was missing something in my life but I didn't know what it was. I honestly never did think that I should be a songwriter. I'd been hurt by comments about my writing and performing and I took them to heart. But it doesn't really matter why I came back. It was enough that I did. I didn't know how much it meant to me until I was re-introduced to my craft. You see the thing about passion and the heart is that we only truly awaken to it when we're doing it. I think it's hard to identify when you don't know what the thing is you should be doing. It's a true expression of the human spirit, the thing that makes our souls sing. I remember the moment I said – I am a songwriter.

What did that feel like? I was so naïve about the process that it never occurred to me that this statement would change my life. Like breathing, it seemed like the natural thing to do. I wasn't aware of what I was getting myself into. There were no preconceived notions about how or why or what. It wasn't until years later I looked up the definition of a songwriter and saw myself in the words.

I look at those early songs now, they weren't very good. I was distilling all of the songs I'd ever heard and writing my own versions of them. It's a good exercise but it has its limitations. I was looking for my voice, something a lot of writers do when starting out. The tunes were derivative, the words contrived, but it was enough that I was trying on other people's music to find the style that fit me. I went everywhere looking for information; how to write, how to sing, how to play – everything. I wanted it all. I had a lot of time to make up for. I flew blind most of the time, but I was open and eager to learn. And there was so much to learn. I begged others to share their gifts and knowledge with me. I found the more I opened myself, the more I learned and the more receptive others were to teach me.

I let the ideas flow through me and to me, and picked up what I could. But I also didn't give up. I kept at it no matter what and vowed to keep going whatever the outcome. That made a difference. I was able to let my personal writer grow up. It's a big concept, allowing one's self to be a writer. It's a choice. Why we as writers limit our potential is beyond me. There is nothing sweeter than the job well done, the lyric nailed, the words exactly as we want them to be. Trying everything and anything gave me exposure. It opened my eyes. Embracing the possibility gave me the courage to keep trying and learning. It was the food I needed to grow.

I took several workshops with Roy Forbes and Bill Henderson. I wrote endless emails in the middle of the night to Stephen Fearing, and he graciously responded to each and every one of them. I held a song circle in my house for a group of writers. We challenged each other and grew. I learned how to listen to the masters of songwriting and embrace the rules and genres that have come before me. I learned how to respect their talent and output. I learned about the balance between music and words, prosody. I learned how to communicate my message to the listener as clearly as possible. I learned about writing in different styles and what each style held in terms of music and words.

Meeting other writers who were at various stages of their own journey amazed me. I saw all the stages I had experienced and some of what was to come. I reveled in their successes. I felt encouraged enough to experiment on my own and truly felt alive for the first time in my life. By asking questions and really listening to the answers I drank from the wealth of their combined knowledge. I was like a giant sponge soaking up everything. It was exhilarating. I began to vibrate to a different way of thinking. Was I really starting to believe that I was worthy, good enough to be a songwriter?

I think the biggest thing I learned was how to let myself TRY. We as human beings don't do that. I don't know why. It's a mindset that serves to keep us shut off from possibilities. As we get older we shut off that "child" that dares to do anything. I had to relearn how to connect with that child. I had to take my heart out and pass it around for others to hold. It's not just about the writing; it's about trusting yourself and others, a frightening thing.

I remember those early workshops. I felt so disconnected. I didn't know what I had in me. But I must admit, I kept at it, like a dog with a bone. It became clear to me very early on that I wanted to do this and I gave myself permission to write. Let me say that again – I gave myself permission to write. Whatever the reason, it was the impetus to keep going. I tried things I would never have done before.

Sometimes I failed, but I was learning how to say – it's okay.

It's enough that I woke up and embraced whatever was to come. Not everyone has the chance or the courage to return. Not everyone has the desire to be rejected and keep going. That's an integral part of songwriting, being rejected in an art form that is so subjective. It truly is "beauty in the eye of the beholder".

Jim Moffatt: I played full time and made a decent living from the late 70's to 1990. Then I fell apart. Wife left me; seemed like music left me too and I went back to school to become a jointer. Carried on that way for a few months, almost a year then moved to Victoria and started playing again. A whitewater kayak accident tore tendons off my fingers and I had to learn to play again. Was doing well and then things happened again.

This time it was a series of car accidents, three. The first stopped me for a few months, the second a bit longer and the last happened right as I was trying to start up again from the second. I know it sounds bizarre but it happened and the end result was I couldn't play or write for a period of three years. That seems like forever. Once I started to play again, it was like learning all over again. Hands didn't work like they used to, fingers didn't bend like they did and I even had to play chords differently.

After two surgeries, the pain was gone enough that I could move and as soon as I touched my guitar....well I just couldn't stop. I am writing, running a songwriters' group in Victoria called Art of the Song and going to my regular SAC writers' group. I have started performing and that is a big deal. I still find it hard to get on a stage again. Put on a ton of weight and have only taken half of it off so I feel real self-conscious on stage. As I type this I am listening and working with a Nashville studio who is recording a new song I co-wrote with John Coswell and a guy named Al. They lay the tracks and then send them to me to add my vocals and guitar to. Gotta love the Internet.

So in total I was away from music for almost 10 years. I am back. I refuse to quit. I will not GO AWAY and I still love it. As a writer, I have a lot to offer and say still, so as long as I feel that way, it's going to happen.

I feel like it has been a battle to get here. To get back. I don't feel like I left so much as I had my tools stolen and had to fight to get them back. I am not tired of fighting yet!

Joanne Stacey: I was born into a musical family and from the age of 5, was singing in the family band. It was what I knew how to do. I made my first EP when I was 27 that included 4 of my own songs and moved through the motions of promoting myself as a country artist in Canada. At this time, it seemed that the face of the female country artist had changed into molding each one into some sort of sex symbol. I was not down with this! While I am not ugly, by a long stretch, I couldn't imagine how I could compete with this ideal that was becoming the accepted norm in country music. I am an artist who values integrity and talent over being sexy. Finally at a music conference, after one radio programmer telling me that he would play my music if I came to his room to perform a sexual favor, I threw my hands up in the air and quit.

After going back to school to become a legal assistant and taking a few years to process my anger, I came to the realization that I couldn't stop being a singer/songwriter/musician any more than I could cut off one of my own arms. It is part of who I am, like it or not.

So at that point I became more serious about the craft of writing, began playing the guitar with more dedication and worked on my overall performance skills, including learning to do harmonies for other people. That is how I met Jane Eamon. I slowly made my way back into the music scene and have grown immensely in so many ways.

Ian Thomas: I have performed as an actor and singer in hundreds of commercials. I have busied myself as a film composer. I am however very aware that whenever I return to songwriting, I am engaged in my true love and passion.

Chapter 12

Am I dooming myself to a life of poverty by becoming a songwriter?

All the things I'd ever learned about the music business and art in general, led me to believe that choosing this kind of occupation was tantamount to living a life of poverty. Not knowing anything about the "biz", I was sure I would have to spend the rest of my life writing songs as a happy pastime.

But I did wonder if there was any way I could make a living. I had no aspirations of selling my songs in Nashville. I honestly didn't think I was going to be picked up by a record label and given instant fame and fortune. But I did hope to devote most of my working life to the thing that made me happy and I looked for some way that I could do this.

It didn't work, at least not at first. I barely made enough at gigs to cover the gas. I didn't have anything to sell so I had to make some hard decisions about recording CDs. The expenses seemed astronomical and way out of my budget. But I began to realize that I had to record, I had to have product to sell and I had to play those gigs in order to be seen and heard.

I worked a full-time job the entire time I was learning how to be a songwriter. Coming home at the end of the day didn't leave a lot of time or energy to devote to my craft. I was resentful of the working life, but grateful for the steady cash.

Over the past year, I quit my job and sold my house. I vowed I would ONLY be an artist and have watched my income drop significantly. I think I've changed my view of poverty vs. art, but it's still a struggle.

A lot of the writers I spoke with do make a decent living being writers. I was curious as to how they managed. It's an interesting contrast between art and commerce. And it does require a balancing act.

Hal Brolund: I think that the act of writing is itself separate from the act of commerce. I think that our best writing, the stuff that really speaks to and moves people, comes from a place outside of commerce. A place that doesn't care if you eat, have good clothes or a big screen TV. It is the place that only cares about the story and the melody and the emotion. So we aren't doomed to poverty as much as free to be connected to the story, the melody and the emotion without concern for commerce.

Andrew Smith: There's enough money to survive (otherwise I'd be dead). And there's always the hope that your song(s) – or even your performing career – might get its "big break" and pay for your retirement. Indeed your songwriting catalogue might maintain some monetary value when it's passed to your children. Who knows?

But yes, in the mean time, I live gig to gig with no "nest egg" for a rainy day – is that poverty?

Yael Wand: You've got to do what you've got to do. Follow your passions with faith, and believe….

Kristin Sweetland: I truly believe this does not have to be so…although I have yet to discover scientific proof.

Ian Thomas: There is no poverty of spirit when one is engaged in one's passion. One may simply need to support that passion by additional endeavors to satisfy physical needs. Somehow in our UN war-based industrial model, if we can't make a living at something we are failures. In its purest sense all art might be best viewed as an expression of soul, a human need. This need can be met quite successfully with no sales component. Hobbies can be good for the soul.

David Essig: It's actually worked out pretty well – I've been one of the lucky ones who has been able to practice the art/craft and keep a roof over my head. I knew when I stopped being an economist in favour of songwriting that I was going to forego a lot of future income and was prepared for life in the garret. So the relative financial comfort has been one of the surprises of my life.

KJ Denhert: This is not at all true. Many folks have built fortunes on a hit song. I truly wonder whether hit songs are fewer and farther between. That would be an interesting study - how much money did the person who wrote Happy Birthday make? I hear it's a lot. There's so much hype and legend in this business – I'd love to see real numbers. Nonetheless, I have never written a song strictly in the hopes that it would be a hit. I hope I've already written a hit that has yet to find its place in our culture.

Mae Moore: If your motivation for writing songs is a monetary one, then I suggest that perhaps you find a new occupation for your time. I say this because it is my view that the most enduring and meaningful songs come from a place that is pure emotion, fuelled by joy, outrage, sadness…the full spectrum of the universal human condition. It is very possible to make money, even a lot of money, from the craft of songwriting, but to have this as the primary goal takes the art out of the process. Bob Dylan, Joni Mitchell, Bruce Cockburn, Gordon

Lightfoot…the list goes on and on…all had something to say that they couldn't hold back. I don't think they were checking in with their inner accountant to see if it was going to be a "hit" and bring them a six figure income, before they wrote the song. Nothing is guaranteed in life except, well, you know the rest.

Shari Ulrich: Actually songwriting can be the most lucrative aspect of music – and I like the fact that there's always that possibility.

I believe if you are true to your creative self and are educated in the "business" of songwriting to some degree; your creative muse can evolve into other aspects of creating music – as in film and TV scoring. But it definitely takes a commitment and intention.

Maria Dunn: Not necessarily true. It just takes time to reap the rewards.

If you write good songs, then other people will want to sing them, maybe even want to record them (mechanical royalties) or pay you for singing them (SOCAN performance royalties) or want to use them for an independent film or TV production and gradually you will reap some financial compensation for your songs.

Sometimes people will hear what you have written and they will commission other songs from you based on your previous work.

I have also had a playwright pay me for using a song that he felt was particularly suited to the subject matter of his play.

So between all these sources of income, a songwriter can start to see a decent chunk of money.

Barry Mathers: My house is paid for and I have two Harleys as a result of writing and playing music.

Jory Nash: Hmmm. I fundamentally disagree with this idea. There is money in songwriting. There can be LOTS of money, there can be some money, there can be no money. It all depends on what kind of song you write and how you market, promote and popularize your songs. Even if you don't write songs that a majority of people know there is still money in songwriting. Within the folk world, one can still have one's songs "make" money through airplay on the CBC, placement in TV shows, playing said songs live in concert where concert royalties are paid. Last quarter I got a cheque from SOCAN for $750. Woohoo! Someday I hope to see a few more zeroes after that.

Plus what is poverty? Proper fiscal management can allow someone to get by with less...so even if I make less through songwriting than any other life pursuit, if I'm careful with my money, I'm no further behind.

Norm Strauss: Yes, stop now before it's too late!

Making a living at writing songs?

So when we pair music with money, is it possible to maintain artistic integrity?

It has always been my belief that songwriting and playing music with original material should be treated as a career with a wage just as any other job. Taking a step back from the artistic side of it, bills still have to be paid and the career should generate enough income to pay for itself.

Sadly, that has not been the case for me. The type of music I write and perform does not seem to lend itself to big dollar venues or radio play. Smaller more intimate venues are the norm and CD sales are small.

So how does one make a living wage doing something you love? Perhaps wage needs to be redefined and taken out of the equation when speaking of songwriting and music.

I agree that writers need to write. It's a given. I have to write songs. It's what I do. It makes me feel better. But I am also practical by nature and wonder often at the value placed on folk music performance.

In my experience, to have a venue pay more than $100 for an evening's work is like pulling teeth. Local is worse than out of town. But how do you value your product (you) to the point where you consistently get the same amount of money for what you do?

What is the value of music? What is the value of your songwriting? If I were to think about the hours and hours spent honing my craft, I wouldn't be able to place a dollar value on what I do. If my music touches someone enough for them to want to purchase my CD, does that have value other than the cost of the CD? If I'm not as good or as flashy of a performer as someone else and get a small crowd to a venue, does my music have any less value?

Of course there are lots of ways of making a living with music, teaching, producing, session work, but that's not really the point. It's only part of it. It's paying our artists a living wage to do what they do – art.

So how does one break through this miasma and make a living?

Career songwriters use a lot of different things to keep paying the bills. One thing I noticed from the writers who answered this question, there was vehemence about making a living and being proud of it. "Suffering for one's art" was not an option and it was treated as a job with wages. I asked if it was necessary to separate the working life part from the artistic part. The responses still had the element of staying true to your art. But how difficult is it to stay true to your art when you can't pay your bills?

Ian Robb: I'd be the first to admit that few professional singer/songwriters could make a living by writing at the rate I write or by not putting their own songs front and centre in performance. I personally think that's regrettable, but that's another discussion.

Andrew Smith: Some people respect me for doing original music, some feel sorry for me. Many are surprised that I haven't thrown in the towel and got a real job by now – given that my music has not made me famous.

The Songwriter's Voice

Musings on Art for Free

I have for the past few years, given away my CDs to anyone who wanted them or sold them at a very cheap rate so folks would buy them. Why? Because I wanted people to enjoy my music. It's that simple.

I've had numerous discussions with people saying, "Why are you doing something so crazy! Shouldn't you be trying to recoup your costs for making the CDs in the first place?" Of course, but that's not why I make music. I don't want to be a business, even though I guess I should be. I want people to listen to my music and get something from it.

[1]People buy Christmas lights and put them up, year after year and no one pays them to do that. It's much like the Internet where people are giving away content for free all the time. You can find just about anything you want on the Internet and more often than not, it's free.

When I play a gig that is poorly attended and I don't sell one CD, I leave feeling like a failure. That's not right. I shouldn't have to equate my worth and artistic value by the number of CDs I sell. So I give them away. I don't want my art to become a monetary pursuit. I think it would suffer. But how does one make a living?

I'm starting to believe that art is its own reward. We do it because we have to. I won't stop writing songs because I'm not making any money, and I won't stop writing my blog or books or playing shows because I'm not making a living. It gives me great joy to be able to share what I consider a gift with others.

---

[1] This section was inspired by a blog from Seth Godin

Chapter 13

What is your definition of commercial? Do you have an edge?

I wanted to find out if "being commercial" was a prerequisite for making a living. In folk music, commercial is really not much of an option. We don't generally sing pop songs, at least I don't. And I don't often sing songs that people know.

As a songwriter, it's vital to my artistic integrity to stay true to who I am and who I'm becoming. I can't negate the things I feel I need to do. Nor can I think of the audience every time I write a song. It would be death to me.

For the longest time, I didn't think I had an "edge". I guess by definition, edge being a penetrating insightful quality that set me apart from everyone else. I felt like all the other songwriters out there trying to get gigs and survive. And there was no way I was going to make a living in that market.

So I decided to stop trying. I decided that it was better for me to stop caring so much what everyone thought of me and start trusting that as long as I remained true to myself, I would survive.

It didn't make the money flow any faster, but it gave me enormous satisfaction knowing I was doing the right thing for me.

Maria Dunn: Obviously I want to make a living at music but I wouldn't have chosen folk music in the first place if I wanted to be "commercial".

An artist who may have set out to make music because they love music may become commercially successful. If so, that's something to celebrate, as it's a difficult business to be in. However, that success, attention and hype can put additional pressure on an artist that makes it difficult for them to be as grounded in the art as they should be (celebrity, recording contract demands or deadlines, more and more people with a vested interest in the artist's product who may put pressure on an artist to "produce" to a certain end). When that sort of pressure starts to interfere with the artist's process, that's when they may get into trouble with making art that isn't as good as it could be.

Lynn Harrison: I think a lot of people use the word "commercial" as shorthand for both "professional quality" and "stylish". They're not the same thing, though both can be key to songwriters' success. I think we all need to be aiming for professional quality, which is to the say the level of craftsmanship and quality in songwriting form. Still there are always new forms coming to light that people find meaningful…which brings us to "stylish". I've always felt that artists are fortunate if their personal style of expression happens to align with the prevailing style of the times. Although we're all influenced by cultural norms to some extent, I tend to think it's wise to stay true to one's own artistic instincts and talents, whether they're "in" or not. Such an expression is inevitably more heartfelt and genuine than one that is self-consciously manipulated to fit into the current trend.

Ian Thomas: Commerce is what occurs when you hook your creative wagons up to the horses of industry. Often it has very little to do with art. It can be a blessing but for most it is a curse. Some invested heavily in the trappings of market can maintain what is called an edge for a slender window in time, but the real edge might reside in believability and talent that is to say, just doing whatever it is that you do as honestly as possible. Trying to have an edge, or thinking you have one, could be a silly diversion from seeking some kind of artistic truth or a delusion of vanity.

Hal Brolund: Having never been "commercial" I don't know if I'd lose my edge. Again this is a question of commerce. A song is neither good nor bad because it sells. One song sells and another doesn't. Both can be good. Both can be bad. The "commercial" one simply resonates at the widest possible level, reaching as many people as possible. From a professional point of view this is a good thing but simply because Wooly Bully was a big success doesn't mean it's a great song.

Kristin Sweetland: Will I lose my "edge" if I AM commercial? I think I entertain this question more often. And I would never think anyone would suggest I haven't suffered enough for my art! I think a better question would be – do we really need to suffer for our art in order for our art to be truly great? Does every masterpiece require a blood sacrifice? Hmm, I am inclined to believe it does, yet am currently trying to convince myself otherwise. Back to the commercial thing –I am convinced that no serious artist or songwriter is immune to thinking about it. We all want to be successful at what we do and it's easy to associate commercial with "success". I guess it's just about trying to continuously remind myself of the great sea of artistic successes that exist in the world…the success of the perfect word, the perfect rhyme, the perfect note and that ultimate moment of "a-ha" when the entire song comes together and you know you have created something magical.

David Essig: I believe that you have to be true to your voice and not worry too much about this one. There's a great deal of extraordinary craft in writing commercial songs, just as there is in writing pulp fiction. And if that's your calling, more power to you. For me, I've just listened to the voice, written it down, polished it up a little and put it out there.

I've suffered plenty but necessarily for my art. If anything, the art has relieved the suffering. I don't know what it means to be commercial – if it means being able to live a normal economic life, then I guess I'm commercial. But I've rarely written anything with the prospect of eventual economic success arising from it. I've written songs on demand for a couple of movies – neither of them paid for a latte at Starbucks.

Shari Ulrich: One can indeed premeditatedly and consciously aim for their music to be "commercial" – I've done it and had success with it. But the music that really reaches inside people's souls is that which I write with no goal or audience in mind, other **than for it to** "work" for myself and the listener. I think of the goal as being to draw the listener in – to cast a spell with the song and take them on a journey. I think the exception to the "commercial" goal being restricting is with film. I love the challenge of translating the visual medium into a song or a score. The emotional power of music plays such a big part in the impact of the scene. Though doing that work has had its own economic downturn, it still can be economically rewarding

KJ Denhert: I want to write accessible music. I never want to be playing over someone's head. I am learning to trust myself more each year that I know what I like and that it's ok.

Gary McGill: I've never been the kind of guy that wakes up in the morning and stares at a chalkboard in an office and says to myself: "Now, what rhymes with 'oh baby'?" Foisting an agenda- driven construct on the vulnerable public is about the most dishonest thing I could ever imagine. I don't do that thing. 180 degrees from Tin Pan Alley.

Barry Mathers: What is "commercial"? I think it's a pretty broad term and to me, it means anything that has a good following. Top forty is definitely commercial, but so are artists like Steve Earle and John Prine who sell 100's of thousands of records but don't get airplay on most radio stations. So it's good to write songs that will appeal to some sector of the listening public. Suffering for your art makes thin soup, which I have eaten my fair share of in the past!

David Borins: If you goal is to write for others to perform, or for film and television then losing your "personal edge" is an advantage. You must be completely versatile and empathetic. If your goal is to perform your own material, you must guard your own voice and "personal edge" above all else. If your material resonates with a growing audience, then your music has potential in the marketplace.

My definition of commercial songwriting would be writing specifically for other artists or for specific situations (like jingles or film music) i.e. the marketplace. I'd personally would ask the question, "Will you lose your chance for success as an artist if you are writing music outside the popular trends?" or "will your artistic capabilities be compromised by writing music for the marketplace?"

Bruce Madole: As far as measuring success in any sense, there have always been some songs and some poems that seemed to me to arise more directly from the deep vein of inspiration and some where I had to sweat over years to keep refining and revisiting the vision that has not yet been clarified. I have had no great commercial success of any kind, so the successes have been of a quieter more reflective nature. I remain one of those writers who has spent a lot of time mentoring others and reflecting on how one might teach something that is essentially not teachable while remaining fully aware that I have very little in the way of a track record judging by more commercial standards.

Lorraine Hart: Let me start with this question…what does it mean (to me) to be "commercial"? Simple…marketable is the answer. That simple answer, however, includes within it the full range of what marketable can mean…the good, the bad….and the awful pretty.

As a performer, the shittiest day in the studio (like recording a commercial for salami) trumps the best day of being a receptionist or slinging beers. You can look at it as suffering for your art or you can look at it as paying dues as a professional…and bottom line, paying rent! I've made a living as a professional, some gigs harder, some easier and many…bloody magic, mate!

Your edge is your edge. You define it. Many think you lose your edge by being commercial. You give away your edge if you make changes to your songs and performance that don't feel right on the simple say-so of a marketing rep. However, if you're contracted to write a song, or you're writing for the market, expect to deal professionally with the commercialism. As everything else in life, it's an oxymoronic tightrope. If you ain't jonesin' to dance on it, get out the way and let someone who is, get up there.

To get wrapped up in these issues is to create tape loops of striving and despair that can only have a damaging effect on our own psyche. Good sells...crap sells...how much are we willing (or pulled by the Muse) to invest in the opportunity to try? There's the epiphany to have and hold.

Andrew Smith: I think the issue is not whether an artist is commercially successful. Commercial success and fame happens to the best and to the worst – just like poverty and obscurity. It's more about whether or not an artist stays true to what they personally want to (or feel called to) do, to say and to create. From an artistic perspective then, commercial success is incidental, neither here nor there.

However, since I'm also an entrepreneur who has to pay the bills, I'm thankful that my music has enough commercial appeal that I don't have to go out and get another non-musician job – though many great songwriters do.

Norm Strauss: I like to always boil it down to the very basics to keep myself sane. I like to write songs. It gives me some sense of purpose and the knowledge that myself and other people seem to enjoy and are sometimes, even deeply affected by some of the songs I write. Become a well-known financially successful writer? Sure, we all like to be acknowledged for our work. But when that becomes your prime motivator to write, then you get into the whole "whim-driven dream" scenario where you can become disillusioned with your art.

Personally I would like to side step that whole thing somehow and keep centered on why I started writing songs in the first place. In its purest form, songwriting is an eloquent means of self-expression and a profound medium for communication. For me, anything else is gravy I suppose…I know there is the all too familiar scenario of the Nashville (not picking on Nashville necessarily) writer who is under pressure to write every song as a hit song. This usually means a song with the widest possible market appeal and a restrictive paradigm for lyric and melody. I think this is when our art starts to suffer and we can get frustrated.

Mae Moore: I started out as a folkie performing my songs in coffee houses before landing a record deal and garnering commercial "success". The transition was both exciting and terrifying as I was not, in the beginning, comfortable with performing but was thrust out on the road to support the release of my first album, "Oceanview Motel" (1990). I felt that I had one foot in the canoe and one on shore, as I was still a folkie at heart, comfortable with small listening audiences, but was expected to play the pop game of song chart position and radio station glad-handing. It was hard. Folkies saw me as selling out and my label didn't think I was delivering what they wanted. After "Bohemia" (1992) achieved success on Triple A radio in the US and charted on Billboard, the label wanted me to deliver another "Bohemia". I gave them "Dragonfly" (1995) instead, a collection of songs that reflected what was happening in my life at that time, the death of my father, the death of my relationship and my steadfast hope in better days. They dropped me a few months after the release. Ironically, "Dragonfly" went on to be awarded a SOCAN achievement for "most played song on radio" (Genuine). This marked the beginning of my days as an independent recording artist. Moral of this story….anything can happen.

Jory Nash: The concept of "suffering for one's art" is pure bullshit to me. It doesn't make my art better if I can't afford to eat lunch. I think Wynton Marsalis wrote an essay on this subject and I agree with him completely. My art can only get better with success in the sense that I can focus completely on it once I have achieved financial independence. The question whether people then still dig it, is relevant, but secondary.

I don't care about words and concepts like "commerciality". If I write a song and no one listens to it for 20 years and then suddenly someone puts it in a movie and it sells 10 million copies, is it suddenly a better tune? No, it simply has a successful time and place in terms of the number of listeners. The tune is the tune is the tune. The artist writes it and moves on.

I am just one little man. And what is edge anyways? My definition of edge might be your definition of smooth. I write songs. Period. People dig them, or they don't. Period.

Jane Eamon: I agree with the suffering for your art stuff. I think you should write for the "right" reasons, thinking about how you're going to sell it shouldn't be in the equation. There's a time to wear the businessman's hat and there's a time to set it aside. I don't think you can write from a "monetary" perspective and write well. Songwriting has to be separate. It can't be coloured with visions of dollar signs. It has to be centered on the task at hand or it's not real.

Having said that, what about professional Nashville writers who write hits for a living? Is that songwriting? Yes, of course it is but the focus is on making a hit not so much on writing a song. Isn't this a little like the theatre vs. movies? They're still original songs. You can bet that there are many, many songwriters in Nashville who are suffering for their art even if that equates to getting a hit song as the end result. Different reasons for writing but still writing nonetheless.

So the outcome may be different but the desire and logic is the same. Songwriting is still songwriting. Maybe it's how you market yourself and your products? Look at someone like Lady GaGa. You might not like her songwriting but she's a product that has been marketed very well and she writes her own songs.

So it might come down to learning about the "business" of songwriting where you write but you also explore as many different ways to market your products to make a living.

Chapter 14

On the music business and staying alive

When I first ventured into the music market, I had no idea what I was doing. I followed the lead of several folk songwriters I admired, and did what they did. Recorded a CD, packaged it attractively, sent targeted emails to radio DJs who might play my music, built a website, played mind-numbing gigs to get seen, played a lot for free, travelled to coffeehouses and small venues out in the middle of nowhere, spent a lot of time on the phone, wrote press releases, talked to newspapers and local media, asked for advice, reviews, criticism, feedback....in other words, I became a one-woman marketing firm. Some of these things were successful, but overall, I'd say it was a lot of wasted time and energy.

I got tired of it all very quickly and felt more than a little discouraged. I wondered if my approach was wrong and really thought long and hard about what I could change and still be effective.

I think the music industry models, especially in the folk world in Canada, are dismal. There are so many folks vying for the same gigs and dollars, that's it's almost impossible to maneuver yourself into a place where you can get the good gigs and get exposure.

My age and relative obscurity may have had a lot to do with my outcomes, but it shouldn't have to be that way. I felt and still do, that worthwhile writers and performers should have a shot at making a decent living. Too often I feel overlooked for the sake of the "latest flavour" of the month. Too often I think my desire to remain true to my real artistic self is a detriment to my career. But there has to be a balance between what I know is right for me and my place in the musical community.

I asked the writers how they managed. A lot of these folks are quite successful but I was sure it wasn't easy. There had to be a common experience amongst us and tricks for coping with the "biz".

Yael Wand: Everything I've heard about the music business is true.... sort of. It does take an incredibly determined individual to make her way through the maze of the music industry. One must have an amazing belief in her own abilities and in her worth as an artist. Funny how it's in such contradiction to the doubts one feels as a writer, and maybe in fact, these doubts stem in part from the nature of the music industry. It's an incredibly competitive industry – pushing for gigs, arguing for better guarantees, trying to get a song played or an album reviewed in print. Yet on the other hand, I've met the most wonderful, helpful people through the industry, and there is a sense of comradery and understanding amongst people who make their living in music. I have my own vision of the kind of career I want to develop as a musician and despite having come across very few working examples of such a career, I believe it is possible, and I believe that I can build the career I want to have. I think it's a fine balance between naivety and clarity of vision that keeps one going in this business.

Shari Ulrich: It's definitely the hardest part of doing what we do. And I find the Internet and the glut of "opportunities" being sold to hopefuls makes it even harder than when you just had to get ONE record label to open the gate for you. However, I still prefer having lots of angles to pursue and more independence. But it does require relentless tenacity and it does wear you down. I think if it's not happening for years on end, it may be time to put your focus elsewhere and play for your own pleasure. Sometimes we have to question WHY we are determined to be "performing" artists. If it's because you have a "gift" that you want to share and you can feel its effect on those who listen, it tends to work a little more easily. But if it's a root hunger for self-affirmation to fill a lifelong hole and insecurity, it tends to affect the performance and content in a subtle way that doesn't draw folks in, in the same way.

David Essig: After 40 years of this, I don't have a very monolithic view of the "business". To me, you just write the songs, record them, get the gigs, play the gigs and then do it all over again. I've never been very competitive about the biz and consequently it's never hurt me very much. I truly believe that competition is the death of art. I've had guys who've opened for me wind up living in the mansion on the hill and that's fine. I don't envy them their success – I'm just happy with mine.

Mae Moore: I am not of the Nashville 9-5 songwriting type. I respect those who can write that way, but it has never worked for me. I do what feels natural and write when I have large open blocks of time available. In this way, I am able to sit with the intention and let things flow for the love of it, not because I am being paid to sit there and think up new lyrics.

Hal Brolund: When I figure that out I'll let you know. The business is difficult, stressful, soul-damaging and tiresome but I am drawn to it. I do what I must to stay alive so that I can play more, write more and be the artist.

Jory Nash: Learn all you can about how to make this job "work". Learn about SOCAN and how SOCAN pays out royalties for songs performed in public. Get your music in the hands of the CBC. Learn to tour economically. Don't drive 300 kms for a $50 gig. Learn about showcase opportunities. Mentor with a more established artist. Diversify your talents and see if you can make money from another side of the business (produce a concert instead of just playing in them). Etc. Etc. Etc.

But first and MOST important: hone your craft, practice your performance, write, write and write again. Learn about grant programs out there and ALWAYS apply for available recording and writing grants. And then when it's time to record, don't skimp on the quality of the recording. A decent recording costs at least $15,000 when you factor in production, mixing, mastering, artwork and manufacturing. Leave some money aside to promote the CD. Don't think about "making your money back"...think about how every CD sold is another potential fan for life. How your CD is your calling card to get your foot in the door to get gigs. And when you DO perform make sure your performance measures up to the CD (and vice versa for already dynamic performers). It is INSULTING to audiences to give them a great performance and an inferior CD. Make sure the performance and the CD compliment each other in style. They do not need to be carbon copies but if you play solo, your CD should not be all full band arrangements.

And then when it's all over, repeat the whole process with CD #2. And so on.....

Maria Dunn: Make sure that music is the first thing that you do in a day (if you can). There's an endless list of the business tasks that can be done, but if you don't feed your muse and your soul by playing and singing every day, then you'll burn out and have nothing meaningful to share when you do get that important gig or opportunity.

David Essig: Well, you have to believe in what you're doing. You have to write to please yourself and then consider yourself fortunate if it appeals to others as well. I'm lucky in that I can pull the tentative listener in with the guitar playing. And it helps the family exchequer to be able to do many things – preferably within your art. That's how I wound up as a producer, radio host, writer, mayor.

I'm not a Labour Economist for the World Bank, pulling down 400k a year – and I don't live in a brownstone on Central Park in New York. Other than that, it's been pretty much a long, sweet ride. I feel I've been successful enough – at 66, I don't think much about this stuff anymore. I just do the work.

Barry Mathers: Diversify. The Cruzeros have three different versions of the band, a three-piece acoustic show for folk gigs and house concerts, a version with drums for larger venues and a five-piece for the big festivals.

Mae Moore: Network and stay true to yourself.

KJ Denhert: Get steady gigs. Be nice to EVERYONE and you'll survive.

Kristin Sweetland: Don't eat the brown acid.

Chapter 15

Is there life after a bad gig?

I've had my share of bad gigs, ones I wished I'd never played. I remember each one of them in vivid detail and cringe over every little thing that went wrong. I can't seem to let that stuff go. I want to be loved and respected. I don't want folks to walk away thinking they've just seen the worst show ever.

I wanted to know if there were tricks to surviving these debacles. Could I somehow learn to forgive myself the mistakes and general faux pas and move on? It's not that easy when you're singing your heart out and things go wrong.

I've played over the sound of the espresso machines, tables scraping across tile floors in the middle of a tender ballad, rain leaking from the roof onto my DI, drunks shouting for Joni Mitchell or Gordon Lightfoot covers while I'm trying to sing a new song, boisterous office parties where patrons want the canned music turned back on...you get the picture.

Then there have been gigs where I cried in the middle of a song and looked up to see the audience on their feet. Sigh....

Shari Ulrich: We always remember the bad ones a lot longer than the good ones. Or the negative comment longer than the positive ones. I don't know why that is – just a quirk of human nature. As far as "bad" gigs go, I make a point of never playing in a situation where folks aren't listening. It's soul-destroying if you're playing original music.

Andrew Smith: I've learned from my friend Norm to try and forget it as soon as possible. One time we were driving out of the parking lot after a terrible gig and I said, "Man, that gig was a painful waste of time and energy" and Norm said, "What gig? I don't remember….."

Yael Wand: Life after a bad gig? The next one. Some of my worst gigs have gotten rave reviews and my best ones gone totally unnoticed.

David Essig: Indeed – only liars have never had a bad gig. You just go back to the motel room, look in the mirror and say, "well, that was that." Then you get some sleep and start over again the next day. "Wake up smiling," as the song goes.

Ian Thomas: Of course. Art is subjective. Some will hate you, some will love you, and some could care less either way. Get used to it if you want to be an artist. If you are bad because of not rehearsing or something within your control, then do the work and life will go on.

Barry Mathers: You are only as good as your last gig and it's something that really gets to me if it was a bad one. Usually the next one is a lot better. We also try and not book ourselves into the wrong kind of gig, which can be disastrous.

Kristin Sweetland: Of course, but sometimes I have felt like I was actually going to die….some of them you get over, some of them you remember FOREVER. We console ourselves by calling it a "growing experience" or a "character building gig" and alas they are. We smile in retrospect. But it doesn't make it suck any less in the aftermath.

Hal Brolund: There had better be.

Maria Dunn: Absolutely – but learn from it. Why was it bad? Was it that you were under-rehearsed or that the venue was not the right venue? Was the sound bad? Was the presenter poor at setting the right tone for your performance? Once you figure that out, then try not to put yourself in the same situation again.

Norm Strauss: I certainly hope so. I have had my share of bad gigs. I am still alive. It strikes me though how after 25 years of doing this, I am still so vulnerable to the factors that can make or break a good gig. If the stage lighting is not just right, or the sound, or the audience too stiff or the wind is blowing from the east instead of the northeast, or someone sneezes during a solo, I don't know. We're all such wimps, aren't we? I mean, think about it. Our sense of success comes from trying to gather as many people into a room as we can and then expect them to give us their absolute attention for two hours while we postulate our theories and strum a six string. Isn't that just a bit weird? A plumber or a doctor doesn't have to worry about anything so grand. Yes, there is life after a bad gig, but be careful, the next one might finish you off.

KJ Denhert: Yes – let it go and don't listen to an entire recording of it.

Jory Nash: When I was younger and more insecure, I would get really high after a good gig and really low after a bad one. I once played a live television show in Toronto and broke 2 strings right off the bat. Worst performance ever and I was depressed for days. Then my sister, who's in advertising, told me not to worry cuz advertising studies show that no one was watching that particular program anyways. Nowadays, I don't have "bad gigs". I may have performances that are somewhat better or worse than others, but in whose eyes? Mine? What if I think I just played the gig of my life and the audience hates it and several people walk out? What if I think I sucked and I sell out of all CDs? Better to simply play, try to take some kind of enjoyment from some aspect of the performance and move on. Plus, the storytelling nature of my performance allows me to follow up a song that I may have made a mistake in with a flawless story. Performances are fluid and changing and evolving...I don't make set lists and I often take requests in midstream. Keeps things fresh for me and adds an element of who knows what.

Some things that can contribute to me not enjoying my own show include the quality of sound onstage and in the house, the set-up of the room itself (I will not play anywhere a pool table is present) weather (more particular to outdoor festivals). Once I was main-staging at a folk festival.....I was all jazzed to play but as I started a HUGE thunderstorm kicked up. Rain pelted the tin roof covering the stage. Audience members could not hear a note I was playing. I played for 25 minutes and all people heard was the rain. I "think" I played well but it could be called a bad gig because no one heard it not even me. Ah well. You just have to laugh and move on. Makes for a funny story.

Mae Moore: We will all experience a less than stellar evening from time to time. Keep in mind, "it's just one night". Tomorrow's a new day.

Lorraine Hart: Of course there's life after a bad gig...probably because we'd really rather there wasn't! There's that wicked sense of humour from the gods again! Have faith, pilgrim, for thy bad gigs, forsooth, will gentle with age into some of thy favourite stories...or fade entirely as thy mind goes!

Chapter 16

WHAT THE HELL AM I DOING? I'm having huge self doubts about this whole business. I believe when the Muse is upon us, we have no choices. We are driven to create, regardless of whether it's convenient or not. How do you deal with the internal editor and self-doubt?

We all have critics, those internal voices that speak a litany of negative words within our brains 24/7. We listen at various times in our lives and they colour every decision we make. We attract them by the very act of listening to them. They can undermine the best of us and they can cripple with astonishing ease. Each of us has our own set of voices. Being creative, I think they are most virulent. They are without mercy.

What is it about the human psyche that attracts self-criticism? Why are we are own worst enemies? We are raised to question our very existence. But in the opening of ourselves to the possibility of being creative, it's almost as if we invite the inner demons to move in and set up permanent housekeeping.

My inner critics are strong. They have beaten me more than once. They can tear apart what could have been a good thing so swiftly that I abandon all hope of ever recapturing it. It has been a very difficult thing for me to go through. It still is. Don't get me wrong, I haven't lost the inner critic, but I've learned to be selective in what I listen to.

I think I must be mad to keep going to this trough again and again. Knowing that I will encounter the demons and critics, knowing I will force myself to jump through the hoops of fire over and over. Knowing I will have to hear what they tell me – you're not good enough, you don't know what you're doing, you're crazy. Arghh!!! At least until a new song comes along. Ah, there's the thing. It's that new song and its limitless potential that keeps me here.

Perhaps the trick is to try on the mantle of positive self-belief. By that I mean, give myself permission to accept whatever it is I do. That is hard for me. It permeates everything I do – this self-belief in my own lack of power. It is a life lesson. I was so used to believing I wasn't – something – worthy, good enough, confident – fill in the blanks. And I paid attention to the demons and believed what they told me.

Tricks for coping? I don't know if there are any hard and fast rules for doing so. Maybe by recognizing that the critics and demons exist and that even though they can be difficult, they serve a purpose. They have their place. I had to learn how to accept them as a normal part of my process. I watched others and learned from their coping skills. I asked lots of questions; I attended retreats for writers and talked with many. I shared my experiences and listened. In the middle of a particularly hard self-confidence war, I tried to sit it out and watch like an objective observer. Easier to say now than when I was in it. But this time it worked. I was able to see what was crippling me.

Sometimes I had to throw in the towel and admit I couldn't face them down. But I always got back on the horse. I never gave up, though folks who knew me at that time attest to my saying more than once that I was chucking it all. But something always drew me back in, the songs, or perhaps the potential for songs. I think that's it. There was always another song to be written. I wrote lots. I kept trying – hammering away at it without thought for the reasons why I was doing it. I let the critics talk to me. I was beginning to see there wasn't anything else I'd rather be doing. And I thought about that a lot. What would happen if I couldn't write anymore? What if the well dried up?

Lynn Harrison: I regard my internal editor as a friend. If an inner voice is telling me that a line isn't quite accurate, or I haven't quite gotten to the heart of the matter, I generally listen and trust that some deeper Wisdom (Great Creator, God....) has a solution in mind that will be revealed if I'm patient enough to keep listening for it. Virtually every time I write a song, I come to a point at which I fear I could be defeated...that I'm not "a good enough songwriter" to pull it off (to solve whatever creative problem has emerged). At that point, I try to remind myself that "I" am not the only creative force at work...and I return to my task at hand. The solution is always revealed. I find that self-doubt and anxiety diminishes when I see my work as being in collaboration with a Creative Force greater than myself. That orientation also helps me when I experience self-doubt arising from the feeling that I haven't accomplished as much in music as I would have liked, or when I find myself feeling jealous of other artists or insecure for some other reason. I try to "turn it over" to a Higher Power. It helps.

Ian Thomas: Ah yes, a life that has no choice but to create something. This is an example of creativity as an affliction. Dealing with self-doubt is an ongoing battle and given the diversity of personality types there obviously can be no singular path to the light of unfettered creativity. Creativity is also not a bottomless pit. It is important to go on input once in a while and listen to, or read what others are doing, or somehow acquire new knowledge. If one is bursting at the seams, stimulated by new knowledge something has to give. Another approach is to work in other fields for a time then return to your passion with joy rather than pressure.

Some unfortunately can't get through the self-doubt. The internal editor is schizophrenic. What sounded wonderful one day can sound horrible the next. This is where the sounding boards of trusted peers are very useful.

Shari Ulrich: I just make friends with it and live with it.

Hal Brolund: Who says I deal with it?

Kristin Sweetland: OMG! I can't even tell you how many times I've asked that very same question while on my knees and shaking my fist at the sky! Once again, I don't think any artist is immune to the self-doubt demons; it's just a question of how adept you are at overcoming it and soldiering on.

Barry Mathers: Self-doubt is the enemy, trying to persuade you that what you are doing is a total waste of time. However, once I have a good song going the doubt usually fades away. As far as the business goes, it's a real roller coaster ride. When we have a song doing well on the radio, or a video on CMT in heavy rotation, there is no doubt but when nothing is happening, it's easy to start second guessing things. We have had the odd critic slam us too and if you let it get to you, it creates self-doubt.

David Essig: This one can be the source of creative bloc. You can't look down on yourself and ask the "what the hell," question. If you think you should keep going, then you keep going. The internal editor should be working all the time, asking the questions: "Does this make sense?" "Is it going to help?"

David Borins: I have two major internal tests that a song has to pass before it's played for a friend or family member (let alone an audience). A: Do I remember the song after it's been written? Do I even remember that it has been written? If not then it will sit untouched or recycled for spare parts. B: Can I completely focus on the moment for the duration of the song's performance? Am I thinking about my grocery list while singing the second chorus? From my experience, performing a good song is like a journey and the focus and dedication to the moment grows more intense as the song progresses. When writing, revising or practicing a new song, I take special note of the "out of focus" moments; these are the places where the song can be improved.

In terms of self-doubt, I figure it's a good balance for those overly confident times. In both cases, it's best to acknowledge the feeling and move on.

Yael Wand: What the hell am I doing? If I only knew. I experience doubts as a songwriter on a frighteningly regular basis, probably most of the time I am not writing. These are so common, that my own doubts are practically part of my writing process: each time I sit down to write I have to relearn how to abolish doubts and fears and endless questions. I'm not sure that I will ever stop asking what the value is of my work, or what my value is as a songwriter. It's almost as though the more I overcome as a performer and writer, the larger the challenges I must overcome when it's time to write again. Maybe each bout of doubts addresses a more ingrained layer of questions.

I find the entire process of letting go of these doubts and questions is a form of Zen, or possibly a communion with something greater than me. I can't "do it" or "experience it" or "get there" all the time, but at the moment when I do let go of my doubts, at the moment that my editor takes flight and leaves me some peace, that's when I am able to create. It takes practice and it takes discipline.

It will probably take me my lifetime to come close to mastering either. But it's those moments which are empty of judgement and fear, that are instead full of possibilities and imagination and beauty that are the reason I am compelled to write. For those moments, it is irrelevant what I have or have not done, who I am or who I am not; I am ecstatic – it's the closest I get to a spiritual experience. And the rest of the time I am a mere mortal, hoping I can get "there" one more time.

Maria Dunn: My path to songwriting and performing my own music came very circuitously. It's not something I could have planned if I tried. That and the fact that I get enough regular feedback from appreciative listeners who tell me that what I'm doing is important and encouraging me to continue, keeps me faithful that I'm doing the "write" thing with my time and energy.

Andrew Smith: The self-doubt is always lurking but if I listen to it, I grow too depressed and despondent to work. I must press on because I don't really have a plan "B".

Jory Nash: I have NO self-doubt. I believe I am a very skilled songwriter who has learned to know about the structure of song. I recognize the importance of melody and know enough chord progressions and techniques to keep writing. I can write melodies that are unique (this is something that is more talent than something that can ever be taught...it is what separates the SONGWRITER from the MUSICIAN, although many people are both). Sometimes I run out of things to say and the lyrics take awhile.

I do however recognize that despite my talents, I may one day have to do something else to make money. Talent does not equal financial success. Look at all the talented artists who died penniless (Van Gogh, Nick Drake). Or were relatively unknown their whole artistic lives. It happens. It might happen to me. We'll see if I can deal with it when it happens. It may already have happened. But I have NO self-doubt about my art. NONE. I'm the greatest thing since sliced bread, but I know that the world may still like sliced bread better.

Jane Eamon: In my early years, I was fraught with inner turmoil. Being such a newbie to songwriting I didn't know it was normal. The more songs I wrote the more those inner voices wanted to be heard. They would question everything I did – right down to the choice of words or chords I was using to write a song. I didn't have the tools to deal with them; I let them get to me on more than one occasion.

I guess the question for me was how much of myself did I want to share. I was pretty good at hiding behind my social mask. It had served me well and now, if I was to get any deeper into this thing called songwriting, I would have to remove the mask or at least move it aside so that others could see my "real" self. A frightening prospect.

KJ Denhert: This is a common question for me. I don't like to get too precious about being a musician. It took so long to accept that this is what I'm supposed to do. Sometimes I feel ashamed because it feels like everyone wants to be a rock star – I want to be proud of what I play and write. I learned that being a star can be a huge pain in the ass and also very isolating. I'm lonely by nature and think that in some ways I've tried to be an anti-star which may have held me back unconsciously. Our culture values being celebrities and knowing celebrities – sometimes I look in people's eyes and I think I see such torment. I remember watching Sheryl Crow and Diana Krall in two particular shows – I thought each of them looked a little miserable. I respect both of these women very much. I don't know if I was projecting what I believe is the shadow side of celebrity onto them or if I am actually that sensitive. They for instance are so good at what they do; I just wanted them to look happier doing it – again it was just in two shows I happened to catch. No one is happy all the time and there's a lot that can happen at a live show to make it a challenge, bad monitors, sound or mix can take the fun out of it.

My thing took me so long that I enjoy myself (when I can hear and have good sound). I deal with self-doubt by practicing focus when I play. Like meditation, I redirect my thoughts back into the note by note – you know just thinking about the next note. When I'm distracted by friends or fans or a personal dynamic and I'm playing a solo I have two tricks – 1. When I get lost or uninspired mid-solo, I begin singing the notes, that's the quickest way to focus for me. 2. If I'm singing and playing I try to hear it like a CD in my head, where my hands and voice are on 5 millisecond delay

I actually have a live video on my CD, "Lucky 7" where I played a song and took a solo while using a looping pedal to play what I had just recorded. When I played a note that I didn't like so much I started singing along. It was so obvious to me and it saved the take. We were on a budget and I knew I needed to do it in one take. With that distraction of singing along, I was able to use my focusing trick. It's the most creative section. I learned this technique from the book, "The Inner Game of Golf".

Lorraine Hart: I would rather live a dream than dream about living. That being said, any writer that tells you they *don't* have an internal editor that questions, or they *don't*

have self-doubt....is an imposter! Dreams don't come without work and they don't come separate from everyday living. If we weren't emotional, we wouldnae be writers! The ups and downs can be more relegated to life and to deal with it......I WRITE.....I MAKE MUSIC. It's a sickness and a cure....a madness and the sanest thing I know.

You can dream about that hit song and becoming rich and famous....but living that dream doesn't have legs for all the variables of the journey, in my opinion, and measuring your success with that dream as ruler will give you an asshole for a self-editor and riddle you with self-doubt.

What puts it back into perspective for me is the privilege of this vocation and community. To dream of always being a part of it...to measure my success in the magic made and played through nearly forty years so far...to think of the talent, love and mutual respect of my comrades-in-arms...this dream sustains me. Whatever I have to do to sustain the dream, I promised years ago. No regrets.

Chapter 17

Bruce Madole on Fear, Despair, and the Darker Emotions

Bruce Madole, one of the songwriters I met online wrote this amazing essay on fear. I asked his permission to use it in its entirety. It's worth reading.

"I had an attack of despair over the weekend. It came on the heels of some really great news for a friend of mine – a serious publisher perhaps taking a serious interest in his songs – and I was absolutely thrilled for him.

No sooner had I hung up the phone, when that little voice began to whisper in my head.

"You're 48 years old," the little voice said, "and you're going nowhere. Nobody's taking that kind of interest in *your* work. Why don't you just face the truth – nothing that you write will *ever* be a commercial success. You are doomed to be invisible. You will throw your days away in half-empty coffee houses and other opportunities of your own making – and all your life will be revealed as an accumulation of delusions like the guano piling up on some deserted ocean island."

Did I mention that the little voice of despair is not particularly kind? Some days it's not so little, either. But it likes to present itself as the voice of objective sweet reason, like a friend that is only after all trying to help us face reality – and whose fault could it be that reality is not kind, anyway?

The Songwriter's Voice

I know that my own creative compulsions are energised, in part, by my ability to deceive myself. (The rest of the time, I just don't give a rat's ass, because I have no choice in the matter.) Unfortunately, sometimes, I struggle with the shapeless, self-destructive voices of my own subconscious.

I know what it means to struggle with depression. Sometimes struggle is the wrong word – as though the ground itself has any choice about gravity, and everybody walking on it, or the inevitable contributions of a hound in the field. However, I have been fortunate not to walk too often in the Valley of the Shadow of "Who the Hell Cares?"

Despair is a tough one, though, because it invites you to examine your expectations about a pursuit that is generally unrewarding in a whole bunch of ways, and infinitely rewarding in others. It asks you to consider, "What did you *think* would happen anyway?" (And, secondarily, "What made you think any of that could happen to *you*?")

In my bookworm childhood, I dreamed of some kind of literary immortality, of writing words that others like myself would enjoy. I hoped and prayed to be published, and to do readings, and book signings. I wanted or hoped to enjoy ... not fame, exactly, but perhaps to occupy an enduring inch or so of shelf-space in the bookstores and libraries of the English-speaking world. I wanted to be, maybe not Shakespeare, but W.O. Mitchell or Dennis Lee, perhaps.

In all my years of writing commercially, I was conscious that doing such work might yield a living, but that it would not satisfy my fantasies of a literary legacy. I've joked about it, too – saying that I don't want my tombstone to read, "Gee, he wrote a great manual".

Underneath the joke was fear – fear that I might never write anything – be it a poem, a song, short story, or whatever – that would endure, that minor immortality I once dreamed of. I just wanted to change the world – is that too much to ask?

Well ... yes. But I'm asking for it anyway.

And so, I fear that I will leave that impossible job undone. I am afraid, too, that if I should by some miracle write such a thing, that it will be consigned to oblivion unseen in a drawer or unheard on a tape. I despair of the work I have already done, and I fear that I will never work again, and I fear.

But then I remember. I remember, once, sharing one of my songs with a performing friend and his manager, and how my song brought tears to their eyes and just broke them up, touching them both in some powerful way, if only for a moment. I am reminded that greatness, or any kind of legacy at all, is not the point of this pursuit.

I remind myself that it is out of my hands how the world will receive my work. I remind myself that what I am compelled to do is to write the best songs possible, and then worry about their commercial exploitation afterwards, using some other part of my brain that is not exercised in the same way (and should not be exercised at the same time).

In the end, I picked up the guitar and the pen again, and I resorted to doing the creative work that I know how to do, trying to find some new way to do it better. The voices of fear and despair remain, like a ghostly chorus, and if I occasionally listen, I will try to let them drive me once again to the music and the words. To my work."

Chapter 18

On writer's block

I've never really had writer's block. I've always been able to find something to write about. However, that being said, my internal critics often prevent me from finishing what I start. They will rail at me about every aspect of my new song until I put it away for another day. But I can always write something. I guess I'm fortunate that way.

But I did wonder if songwriters who rely on new material to make a living ever experienced a stopping of the flow, that moment where things didn't come anymore. How did they cope with that?

Shari Ulrich: I can dance around it for months. But essentially I have to be alone, tie myself to the instrument and take lots of walks with a recording device and utterly force myself to be creative. Fortunately it always seems to eventually work.

Jory Nash: I've never really had writer's block. I've had times where everything I've written was shit or at best substandard. But eventually something good gets finished. Perhaps I've been lucky. Perhaps I just know now when NOT to write. When nothing good is coming out, I put down the instrument and go do something else. Tomorrow is another day.

Mae Moore: I paint, I garden, I ride my bike, listen to my favourite music, cook or bake, knit, clean the house and be gentle with myself. I know that the Muse will come back once I have reframed my state of mind.

David Essig: Just ignore it and keep on going. It happens to everyone and in my world this problem is in the realm of the paradox of duality: you can't push a string, you can't chase the Muse. But you can make a habit of doing something substantive with your art each day and not worrying about whether today's the day you create the masterpiece.

Ian Thomas: Output. Output. Even if it's crap, keep writing. This way one is in position for incoming; those songs that just appear. This is a spiritual thought of a sort, but the metaphor has some resonance with many writers. The stream of infinite possibilities is there. It is the access that is often difficult. Sometimes writing with someone can help you paddle out.

Yael Wand: First I have to convince myself to stop procrastinating. I have to make time. I have to stop hiding from my guitar and start inhabiting my old writing room. I start with small steps: just a few minutes a few times a day. Then I start writing really dumb songs, as dumb as I can make them. At the moments of my worst writer's block I give myself permission to write a series of really bad songs and lyrics, and I allow myself to steal and borrow from whatever I can. I make an agreement with my internal editor that I can let out all the clichés, bad ideas, and general crap or anything else that sounds utterly stupid. I invite all this out and out loud, but always in private…. and without fail, good ideas follow. Suddenly, I'm writing.

KJ Denhert: I never ever force myself to write – I tell myself it'll come when it's time.

Hal Brolund: I read, I listen, I watch a movie. I do anything but obsess about the fact I haven't written. That sounds good except that when I'm not writing it hangs in the air like a pregnant elephant. I am stuck feeling like a song is about to fall upon me at the moment but it is stuck. So I read, listen, watch a movie but I keep a pen and paper close by and hope that the baby comes soon and is not still born by the trappings of life. I try to stay open and ready so that when the Muse feels ready I can write.

Maria Dunn: I immerse myself in the topic that I'm writing about and wait for ideas, turns of phrase to surface. I force myself to take my fledgling ideas and go for a long walk with the main purpose to sing what I've got so far and work my way through it. I play some music that's unrelated or something else that I've been working on; that at least gets me to the guitar or piano and keeps the music flowing.

Kristin Sweetland: First tequila and marijuana. Secondly writhing, moaning and tearing of hair. Thirdly, forcing myself to sit down and work through it. Just do it. Hiking, climbing statues and crying are always helpful. Fourthly prayer, if it comes to that.

Barry Mathers: Wait it out or spark one up.

Lorraine Hart: Being a natural woman (but not *that* woman) and now semi-retired from the commercial machinations of "The Bi'ness" in New York, I feel that I can honour more the ebb and flow of writing. Sometimes it's a simple matter of stepping away for a few....going to sleep or taking a walk. Sometimes I have to let my brain flow in a different way, so I'll draw or paint, read or listen to someone else's music.

When I was working in a very productive writing partnership and under more of the commercial "gun" as it were, hitting the wall in writing marathons meant one thing....time to hit a restaurant and chill for awhile...time to laugh and talk, vying for the craziest gig stories. By the time we'd get back to the studio for another "straight eight" somebody always produced something to cook in the pot and I'd be driving home listening to the demo.

****

In one of the many email conversations I had with Stephen Fearing, he wrote me this lovely essay about dealing with writer's block. It was very helpful and I asked his permission to use it here.

Stephen Fearing: When you're feeling blocked or when the ideas seem "trite" or "old hat", you need to go deeper. Is there a central image, place, person, thing, feeling, or philosophy to the blocked song? Do this, write it on a piece of paper, at the top of the page. Now free-associate. For instance, your central image might be BUS; free-association may net the following words - diesel, Greyhound, betting, money, dirt, dust, prairies, wheat, cereal, milk, cookies, sugar….etc. The point is that you need to get past some block and there are a million ways around it, but you have to find just one. It's mostly about perseverance and the confidence that you will find a way. I would say that this is a good thing, kind of like when you go to your homeopath because your back is covered in hives and they take a look and keep muttering "good, good, good". What's so good about hives? Well a homeopath looks at hives and sees an internal problem that has surfaced and is therefore being dealt with by that wonderful organ – the skin. Hives mean that your body is working like it should be. Writer's block may mean that you're growing tired of your old patterns and the current set of hoops that you jump through when you create a song…it may be highlighting the fact that you have a "set of hoops" when perhaps you should be tossing out the old routine and stepping onto the stage without a set list.

As writers we have to live with our own bullshit on a daily basis and to make matters worse, we have to examine it up close. Nothing drives the creative muse away faster than the hint of stagnation. Remember, boredom is fear, so what are you scared of? Dig deeper. It's like diving and most divers get bored with paddling around in the shallow end. Pretty soon they're diving around wrecks and going deep to get their kicks. The nice thing about writing is that you can't really get the bends. When I say deeper, I don't necessarily mean you should write songs about your sad-assed childhood and how you never got picked for basketball…(feel free by all means), no, going deeper means looking for ways to entice that excitable skittish muse back into your den.

Have you fully explored all the ways to illuminate the image of a night sky? Perhaps you need to stop trying to write songs about specific things and start writing songs about topics that present themselves during the writing…. perhaps you need to stop writing songs period…just start writing and then see where it goes. Make it a daily practice, 15 minutes a day of straight writing. See where it leads you. Don't be so impatient. Don't be so judgmental, it's not math. It doesn't always make sense and it sure as fuck isn't LOGICAL!!!! You are trying to use a different part of the brain. Give it time and give it energy. Don't be worried that you are going to disappear into touchy feely land.

Chapter 19

The Rituals of Writing, how do you get started? Do you have tricks, rituals, favourite pen, computer, spot in the house? Do you follow forms and structures? Do you ever break the rules? Do you believe they have validity?

I think for me the most difficult thing to learn was how to write in a way that communicated exactly what I was trying to say, clearly and authentically. By using my litmus test of tears, I was able to learn how to recognize when something was correct and true for me, then hopefully true for those listening.

But it's not easy to write clearly. Too often I think we try to write with beautiful words and metaphors that one would never use in real conversation. And it's a hard lesson to learn. Someone once told me to stand in front of a mirror and read through the song out loud. Listen to how the words feel without music. Would you say those things in real life? Do they sound forced, contrite, clichéd? It's good advice.

But words are only part of a good song. The music and how it flows around the words can make or break a song. I believe that somehow the music I choose for a song can bring my words to a deeper level, communicating to a listener the depths and colours of my stories. I had to learn that. I had to learn my limitations as a musician and again, give myself permission to accept my skill level and work within its parameters. I'm so grateful that I surrounded myself with musicians at all skill levels who shared their talents and expertise. I listened to their styles and tried to emulate what I heard. I learned later this is genre writing. My rituals for writing are pretty simple, I like paper and pen. I especially like paper I can rip out of notebooks and scatter all over the floor. I do write on a computer and sometimes it's a lot of fun, just stream of consciousness stuff. But I don't have a favourite spot or a special pen or a certain time of the day. I write whenever I can and wherever I can. It's not really that predictable.

Yael Wand: I am a notoriously erratic writer. I can go for months writing every day, working on new tunes or editing old ones. Then I can go for an entire year and write nothing. I've come to learn that I do have a writing switch: it turns off very easily, with the slightest bit of busyness or neglect. But turning the writing switch back on can take months of preparation, planning, cajoling and procrastination. It always switches back on and this fact never ceases to amaze me. I sit myself in my favourite room in the house, close the door and start to make some noise. Sometimes a good walk or just the act of forgetting about wanting to write brings on a line or a full chorus, and then the switch is back on.

Shari Ulrich: I sit down with an instrument and go for a long walk. That's pretty well my one/two combo approach. I don't write lyrics on a computer. I use a little digital recorder that I carry everywhere and go home to my spiral notebooks and write it down the old fashioned way - with a pencil!

David Essig: Noodling on the guitar and long-distance driving do it for me. I tend to write more away from home than at home – don't know why – maybe it's the comfort zone thing.

Kristin Sweetland: It will often take me hours to get into the zone. Being alone is key for me and creating atmosphere. Sometimes I just stare at a blank page or the sky or listen to audio books and scribble until I get a great line. This is when I am TRYING to write as opposed to having a song just descend upon me from the universe. That will happen when I least expect. Always.

Maria Dunn: My preferred way of getting started is sitting down at the kitchen table with scrap paper and pen in hand. There are times when I haven't been afforded the luxury to wait until inspiration hits (song commission deadlines) so then I make myself go for a walk and force myself to try out lyrics, melodies under my breath as I walk. Sometimes I'll take a tape recorder. This has also worked when I've had a deadline and been on a long drive by myself. Again, I'll force myself to try out lyrics, melodies with the tape recorder on (and my eyes on the road!). Then later, I'll be able to shift through a few ideas and see what's worth keeping and working on.

KJ Denhert: I'm most inspired when I have to leave. I write more songs 10 minutes before leaving the house than any other time. It's a bizarre quirk but having accepted that I am getting a lot more done. A recent trick is an MP3 recorder that is really easy to use.

Andrew Smith: When I co-write it's easy to get started – you don't have a choice. You've got three hours, so get to work. On my own, I just play for my own enjoyment and often I get a cool original idea – lyrical and musical – that sets me to the task of chasing down and harnessing and crafting the inspiration into a song.

Yael Wand: I've experimented with all sorts of modes of songwriting. Songs have come from personal experiences, intimate thoughts or emotional struggles. Songs have come in floods of a few minutes and they've come from months of slow and tedious working and reworking. They've come from a desire to deal with a very specific topic, from the idea of creating a certain mood, or from a line that sounds great and a random storyline that just fits. Songs have come from trying to remember a few new guitar chords or from wanting to broaden the scope of my performance repertoire. Some songs are written for no one but myself, some songs are written to say things I can't say. Sometimes I have to change a line to hide the truth and sometimes I change a line to be truthful. I've known some songs will be the audience favourite the moment I've finished writing and at other times the success of a song sneaks up unexpectedly, in studio, or in performance after performance.

For some time, I believed that songs had to come from a specific kind of place, perhaps addressing a burning human question or only from an experience I personally had. As my writing has developed I found that approach limiting and instead have allowed myself to write songs for many different reasons, and I've learned that the song's value does not stem from its source alone.

Barry Mathers: The legal answer is usually listening to some good music to get inspired; the other one involves rolling papers. I always write in pencil, in scribblers and do a lot of erasing.

Joanne Stacey: When I first began writing songs, I had only my voice and the music in my head so I had to work really hard with the melody to make sure it was truly encompassing all the feelings the song was meant to portray. After many years of frustration trying to get others to "hear" what was in my head, I decided it was time to learn to play the guitar. That was, and still remains, one of the hardest things for me to do. To play and sing as if it is easy and I am one with my instrument is a struggle, but it is worth it. My voice will always be my first instrument and I still often begin writing a song with only my voice. When that happens, I will eventually pick up my guitar and work out the options musically as far as where I want the melody to take me in the bridge or how I want the groove to feel. During these times, I pull out my handy digital recorder and this has been a lifesaver! Sometimes during the process, you spew out some great line or melody and then forget what you did. Now, I can go back and find that little magical moment!

Jory Nash: Interesting questions…I usually get started when the mood strikes me. Sometimes to shake things up I try to force it, often with poor results. In the past I have had favourite writing paper and pen (blue rollerballs, medium tip!). But once I got complacent and repetitive, I switched to just writing on the computer, again with mixed results. I'll try something else next, again to see if something new comes out. So to sum up, I do have a comfort zone where I like to write (and what with) and I'm currently consciously trying to do anything but the comfortable thing.

Ian Thomas: Any way, any instrument, any starting point. I begin the process usually with an arranging program on computer so I often arrange as I write. This way I can hear what I'm thinking. Rules are often for breaking provided instincts dictate enough satisfaction with structure, which is the ultimate goal. Is the piece a satisfying entity? If it lacks something in structure it is usually obvious. What came first the song or the rules? Probably the song and then some academic came along trying to understand it. So if the rule doesn't fit what you hear in your head, the rule may be wrong for the piece. If it works well for you, some academic will come along and make a new rule.

Andrew Smith: I have quite a few songs that are approached in what I consider to be a painterly way; that is

I'm attempting to solve certain creative problems in order to be a better writer – and presto, out pops a pretty decent song. For example, I wanted to create stronger and more distinct melodies, so I set myself the task of writing a song with the same progression all the way through. So the only way to differentiate verse, chorus and bridge would be the melody. It would seem a rather academic way to approach a song, but it became the first song on my The World Has Windows CD.

Writing and completing a good song is so satisfying – like having great sex. I think of the Bruce Cockburn lyric to describe the afterglow: "an empty head and a messed-up bed, I'll be floating just above the ground."

Mae Moore: I have to be alone and uninterrupted for a whole day. I write with my acoustic guitar and always use paper and pencil.

Jane Eamon: I've played piano, I've played a drum, I've used capos on the guitar, I've sung without instruments. They all served to carry me in different directions.

It's worthy to say here that I was learning how to connect with that inner "child" that was not afraid to try new things. It's so vitally important to do this. You don't have to be a great musician, but I think the more you learn, the more you can do. It's like the toolkit that always has the right tool for the job. And anything you can add to that kit helps. It's the potential that makes it so exciting.

Lorraine Hart: When I write....I'm gone, baby, gone! I write in a very visual sense, that is to say, my mind's eye is focused either on the movie of the song with words or focused on this great imaginary band that works the music. Obviously both have to have the Copa Cabana imaginary scene where words, music and an audience come together…but that's further down the line of production. If a melody comes first, I have to wait until a picture suggests itself, within that melody. If the words come first, their rhythm will begin to coax a melody. Glory Hal et Lou if both come together! Until they are properly arranged and recorded, they play incessantly in my brain.

I had an incredible experience when my band was hooked up to a computer in an Art Gallery for a mixed media show. It turned all our audio into a kinetic painting as we performed. That was definitely a night through the looking-glass for this very visual Alice! That video is probably the closest thing I have to a "map" of my songwriting process.

Jane Eamon: Bill Henderson once said in a workshop that everything you can learn about the rules of writing and playing will serve you well in your songwriting. I grew up listening to old standards and operetta. I've said that I began writing by emulating what I heard. But my musician skills were not at the same level. I had to learn how to stretch as a musician. I also had to learn the rules of songwriting. The rules are there for a reason. We as listening creatures are drawn to certain forms and structures within a song and will naturally gravitate towards them. That does not mean the rules can't be bent or broken. But they do provide a great wellspring of inspiration and guidance no matter what level you're at.

Shari Ulrich: For every "rule" in songwriting there is a GREAT song that breaks that rule. But I think it's extremely valuable to understand why things work and why they don't. Then I learned that the things I did instinctively had names and reasons I could convey to other people. But I still tend not to think about them when I'm writing.

Lorraine Hart: Not being classically trained on any instruments or in music theory has both its pros and cons. I am dependent on a partner who can help me translate the band I hear in my head to a real arrangement but I can hear and sing the different parts, knowing the right chords when I hear them. This also helps me think a little outside the box....and nothing moves forward without breaking the rules a bit. What's wrong with a ten-bar phrase or the twelve and a half bar blues? I can drive some musicians mad...until they let go, something shifts and they feel it...and suddenly, it's pronounced cool. It is important to learn rules and form before you throw the book out though and I spent years listening, watching, asking questions and learning through osmosis before stretching the envelope in my own writing.

KJ Denhert: I'm sure that I break rules more often because I don't know them. I learned the rules of music similarly to the rules of grammar. When I first learned grammar often I knew the correct answer but not necessarily the rule per se – I had memorized the sounds of correct usage. It's kind of similar with songs. I write different styles now and then, like a reggae tune, or an Americana type of presentation. It becomes a bit of a template but my ears solve things – similarly to the way I would choose to say – "No, I didn't see the show", or "No, I haven't seen it". Both mean the same thing. When to use "see" and when to use "seen" are based on grammatical rules. I speak English by ear, practically unconsciously. I see an analogous situation in completing a new song.

I hear movement from chord to chord and think of the melody as a thread that holds the piece together. A melody refers to rules within the chord; occasionally breaking a rule makes a statement too. I heard a notable rule break in an Edie Brickell song whose tag is "What I am is what I am is what you are or what" It would take me about ten minutes to break down the chords and the melody and define which two notes I believe break the rules, or create a rub. And then after a while I hear it naturally.

There are a lot of principles of perception that I love about a song. I want my songs to have those connections for folks who happen to hear those things. I also want it not to matter because there are lyrics and tempo, dynamics and so many tools in the toolbox, colours on the palate. When you improvise you <u>are</u> rewriting something, often the melody.

Lately I am trying to write melody first – single note melodies then find the chords and a few substitutions to colour the tone basically making a melody happier, sadder, lighter or more serious and everything in between.

Barry Mathers: I don't really follow rules but there are certain boundaries I stay within. I guess I learned what I know by listening to music all of my life.

David Essig: My songs tend to follow the traditional structures of the genres I grew up with. And then I'll bend them a little. They're not so much rules as forms – and I play around with them all the time. In the genre of two-verses-and-a chorus, I've written songs with no choruses and others where the whole song is a chorus.

Jory Nash: I am a believer in song structures, but there are many, many kinds of acceptable structures. I try to employ a lot of them, again to keep my writing from stagnating. Also I sometimes write instrumental breaks and they can be over the verse or chorus or both depending on the song. Sometimes the instrumental break is a completely different piece of music meant to change the pace of the tune.

Sometimes I write in conventional 12-bar blues structure and may or may not write a bridge.

While I believe in writing in form and structure, sometimes tunes take on a life of their own. It is not "breaking the rules" to try something different. I do now believe in rules, per se. They are more like guidelines. In the end a song is successful or not only in the ears of the writer and the listener. Structure be damned.

Maria Dunn: I don't have any hard and fast rules. It depends on the song. I do try and give the listener a repeated refrain or chorus that they can "hang their ears on" or go away from listening to the song with some words and melody already planted in their brain after one listen.

I use a lot of different styles of folk music as models, so they provide a large choice of possible structures. I learned by listening to traditional folk songs and my favourite songwriters. It was years before I ever wrote a song with a bridge and still have only a few of those.

I try to serve the song with the structure. I don't try to make something complicated for the sake of complication. I usually keep things pretty simple in terms of chord structure and form.

Kristin Sweetland: I find structures helpful after I've already written quite a bit. I need to get as many ideas and parts down as possible before I start limiting myself at all. Then creating a structure from the amorphous mass of verses and choruses in front of me is the ticket to actually making a song. This is often challenging and torturous or sometimes very obvious – but so rewarding and absolutely crucial to the success of the song.

Andrew Smith: I think I have too many rules, so I try to break free sometimes and this has resulted in some real growth as a writer. When I hear my son, Zachari, write songs, I always wonder at how fresh they sound – it's delightful to my ears and soul – because he's not bound by the same songwriting rules.

Writing in genre style. Do you work in specific genres? Do you ever challenge yourself to write outside your comfort zones? How do you do this?

I love writing new styles of music; I'm not always successful but the mere effort of trying it on for size makes me happy. I've dabbled in a lot of genres and I've found that my writing has changed over time quite a bit.

I once did an entire CD project where I challenged myself to write my take on very traditional forms – Woody Guthrie, old-tyme gospel, spirituals, Celtic, Gordon Lightfoot type folk songs, anything that felt like roots music. Not today's roots music, more the beginnings of folk music. I loved that project. I got to play in a lot of different rhythms and song structures and I think it helped me grow as a writer. I wasn't relying on the old tried and true of what I'd always done. I was looking to push the envelope.

These days I don't really care what genre I write in. I'm more interested in what's evolving in my head. Sometimes it feels like I've got a whole crowd of folks up there just waiting to get something out or down on paper. And if they want to sing trip hop, ok, so be it. Doesn't have to be good, right?

Jory Nash: Excellent questions! For me, it's important to write in different musical styles. I like a lot of different styles of music and therefore I write different styles. The commonality is my vocal style, but I play several instruments and I'm conscious of writing differently on each instrument. On guitar for example I write strummers, finger pickers and pull and slap styles. All different vibes.

I write blues tunes, jazz tunes, folk tunes, pop tunes, country tunes. I write what I feel like writing and have been praised and criticized for making CDs that are stylistically eclectic. No matter.

Right now I'm trying something different and that is to write 8 different tunes simultaneously working on each a little bit at a time. It's been interesting and somewhat fruitful but not something I will do again. I lose focus on each tune too quickly and they're taking much longer than I'd like to finish. But I'm also coming up with some things I wouldn't have if I'd written them each separately.

Shari Ulrich: I write what I feel and sometimes push myself to try new things, but not genre-specific. I find that it ends up sounding too contrived and trying too hard.

Barry Mathers: I get inspired by listening to other artists and sometimes will write in that genre.

David Essig: Well, I grew up in the parallel universes of Bluegrass and Delta Blues, so I tend to write with one foot in each of those traditions. Because I write inside and outside of the traditions at the same time, I'm always feeling outside of the comfort zone – pushing the definitions a little. John Hartford is a great hero of mine in this regard.

Maria Dunn: I work in a few genres (bluegrass, country, folk, Celtic), but have challenged myself to write some other kinds of songs for song commissions (coming up with more West African rhythms for a song about refugees and immigrants). However, it's all still basically roots/folk music at this point.

KJ Denhert: I always want to get outside of what I think people expect of me, of course that is a projection anyway. I try to listen to things in my head as though they already exist and my brain is just like a radio tuning in a signal.

Kristin Sweetland: I write in the Sweetlandish genre....it is certainly a hybrid of sorts. I think challenging one's self to write in different genres is an amazing experience. You never know what you're going to come up with! I wish I did this more often....I so need to write a hit country song, stat.

Lorraine Hart: I've written in many different genres, on purpose...and also by surprise. At this stage of my life, I like to think that all the genres I've worked in have produced something that is all my own....just outside the boxed definition of any one genre.

Working as a commercial writer did make me fractious to break out of the box of "I love you – I hate you – come here, go away" songs. I felt like I had to sneak issues into the form of love songs.....but this helped me to learn to lyrically give songs layers of understanding potential, without expecting listeners to go exactly where I go with them. I'm sure Sting wasn't about to give back all the money "I'll Be Watching You" made as a love song because he was actually weaving a story of a creepy stalker...and it didn't change anyone's mind when he spoke about it in interviews; they still used it for their wedding day in droves.

I left the commercial bi'ness to give my writers' voices the "pauper's freedom" and, in doing so, have felt the mad joy that freedom brings in new life chapters. That doesn't mean to say I no longer write about love...it is the river that life flows in...but I feel free to age it with deeper meaning or let it disappear into the very fabric of a song's tapestry. I feel free to follow the Muse and craft the voices with my own voice. The delightful surprise that's come along with it is more work and welcome, supportive, faithful audiences.

Hal Brolund: I just write me, whatever that is. Lately it sounds more country. It used to be rock/pop, then blues and now roots country. It's the same music with the same 7 notes. Genre is a function of commerce, not of creation. I don't think in genres when I write.

Joanne Stacey: I truly enjoy writing in many different genres and have pretty much written songs in every one of them at one time or another, either for a writer's circle challenge or just on my own. I just let the Muse take me where it wants me to go! One of my pet peeves about being an artist/songwriter is how everyone likes to put you into a box and they will tell you that it is the kiss of death to put more than one genre on your album. I say, "screw that". Music is music and if all we were allowed to eat was chicken, day in and day out, how boring would that be? It is good to throw a little steak or fish into your diet from time to time too. It's about balance and being true to yourself. Keep 'em guessing!

Ian Thomas: ...changing genres can often take one out of one's "comfort zone". Any good song can be done as a polka or a ballad. Arrangements/genres might simply be how one can dress something up for market. Even Gordon Lightfoot`s "If You Could Read My Mind" has been converted to dance genre. It could also make a good polka.

Chapter 20

On recording and producing, most of you have done multiple CDs. How do you feel about hearing the sound of your own voice? How do you feel about recording? How do you choose your songs?

I love recording, I didn't at first, but I do now. I love the possibilities being in the studio can bring. I love trying out new songs in new ways and hearing the results. I love the sound of my voice when it's recorded well. I love working with musicians I would never get a chance to otherwise. I love what a finished CD looks like. I love designing the packaging. I love the whole CD birth process.

In the beginning, I was so scared to record. I felt like an outsider when people talked about CDs and recording and this studio vs. that studio. It was a foreign language to me. I never thought, in my wildest dreams that I would end up recording 6 CDs and wanting to go back for more!

My first experience in a studio was painful. The engineer basically set the levels for my sound and left the room. I was left to record all my songs on my own with no validation from the booth as to whether they were any good or not. I had no idea. I remember feeling very amateurish and naïve.

I was so fortunate to meet a great producer/engineer – Andrew Smith. He patiently guided me through the process and never made me feel like I wasn't good enough. There were some technical logistics that I had a hard time with, like click tracks and overdubbing and separating my vocals from my guitar playing, but overall it was a great experience. I learned how to listen to my own voice with an objective ear and that's a very good thing indeed.

Over time, I've come to understand what I need in a studio setting; the ability to play and sing at the same time and still have it sound great. That's my most important requirement. Separating me from my guitar is like cutting off my arm!

But the unknown is always fearful. That's why it's the unknown. Sometimes you just have to jump off the ledge and trust you ain't gonna fall!

Yael Wand: Thankfully I've learned so much from each time I've gone into the studio and I love the experience. It's grounding and exhilarating to record and listen back; it always shows my weaknesses as well as my strengths and it forces me to come to terms with my work. I learn more with every recording experience. I don't think there's anyway to learn this stuff except from actually doing it – it's an experience that cannot easily be reproduced, the act of recording one's song and performance for posterity.

I'm getting better at planning out what I want to achieve in the recording of a song or of an entire album, but I still have so much to learn about how exactly to express and to achieve my vision. I'm learning to be a little bit less of a perfectionist: there are things that I hear right after recording a song and listening back in the studio that grate painfully. Yet, a few months later, I don't hear them at all. I hear the song for what it is... hopefully a beautiful engaging experience of several moments.

Shari Ulrich: I love hearing the sound of my own voice! (Is that wrong?) Though I should clarify, I hate the sound of my speaking voice. I have never had the luxury of having more than an album's worth of songs to choose from, so I pretty much record everything I write. I love recording, though for a person like me who hates making decisions, the endless decision-making is challenging. But it's a whole other dimension of the creative process with music that is a great adventure.

Hal Brolund: I used to hate the sound of my own voice. I think that was when it wasn't very refined or polished. I would listen to a track and say – "sounds good but it's only me." Later as I became used to my voice and more skilled at using it, I began to no longer notice it in that way. I hear the music and not me singing it.

Kristin Sweetland: Hearing my own voice is always intense….sometimes I absolutely love it, sometimes I cringe. I very rarely feel nothing. Recording is an incredible process and I LOVE it – it is always a rollercoaster wrought with adventure, turmoil, anger, self-doubt, agony, love, joy and the ultimate angelic euphoria of victory that is necessary for any true mythical journey of a bard. The songs are chosen because they are not just songs unto themselves…they are chapters in the story that is the Album. They fit together and tell a story. They are one.

Jory Nash: I like the sound of my own voice. I didn't at first now I'm used to it. I know what I want to hear when I record and I know when I don't achieve it.

Recording is fun, stressful and costly. I always wish I had more time and money to make CDs. By the time I finish recording invariably I'm tired of my own record. This is simply because I will have heard it literally a thousand times between recording, mixing and mastering. If I had to listen to ANY album in my CD collection a thousand times, I'd be tired of it too.

I choose songs that seem to go together best, to flow into each other and make a complete album. I've never done a "concept" album where the songs are all tied together musically and lyrically, but might do so one day. Occasionally a recorded song will not measure up to the version I hear in my head and I will have to scrap it even if I planned for it to be on the album. Sometimes the recorded version of a song surprises me and is better than what I had hoped for. And then when the listeners hear it, invariably they have opinions about the tunes that are quite different than my opinions.

KJ Denhert: So often I don't actually like my voice when I hear it. I think it's got to sound completely different to somebody else. I let myself get used to it. Recording is great when it's working and hell when you become too analytical. Especially when I am playing the guitar without the distraction of singing, I have to do things mentally to divide my focus and stop trying to do things perfectly. This is the hardest part. It requires the most discipline. Some folks are great in the studio and others great live and there are the mighty few who do both so well. Of course I seek to work with those mighty few people – always wishing I had more skill writing and notating music.

David Essig: I just put up with the fact that I have what some listeners regard as an unpleasant voice and then go for it. I hope that the musicianship and performance will carry the day and listeners won't dwell too long on the fact that I'm no Frank Sinatra. I love recording – not a surprise, given the amount of it that I've done. Early on I was led to believe that it's an entirely different art form from performing, but within a few years of recording/producing I came to the realization that it's all the same. So I see recording as capturing good performance – in fact, a performance that is SO good that it works, even when the listener cannot see you.

Ian Thomas: Never liked the sound of my own voice. It has just been handy when I write the demos. I usually write enough songs for a CD and then quit. I don't finish ideas that don't feel good so usually by the time I have an album's worth of songs; I generally like them enough to follow through.

Barry Mathers: I have gotten used to hearing my voice on recordings and there are even a few tracks that I like. Usually by the time a record gets to the mastering stage, I have heard the songs so much that I'm sick of them and won't listen to them for quite a while. I love recording, especially nowadays because we can do a lot of it at home. It's usually quite obvious which songs are going to make it onto the record.

Maria Dunn: I love recording with people I trust to tell me if a performance is good enough. I've been fortunate to work with people that are both critical listeners with high standards but supportive and respectful at the same time.

It's very important to have that atmosphere in the studio; therefore it's very important to find a producer that you respect and whose judgment you trust and who respects you and knows your music and will serve what you are doing already in the best way possible (rather than take what you do and force you to go in an unnatural direction for you).

It can be very frustrating at times, if you can't quite get a part right, so even more important to have the support of the people around you in the studio. Never hurts to take a break. And it always takes longer than you think so even though the money clock may be ticking, try not to feel rushed. In the end, a few hours of studio time is nothing compared to cringing when you hear something that you've spent thousands more to press into finished form, etc.

In the past, I've chosen songs that have often worked their way up through the ranks of the live material that has been honed over a few years of performance.

With the upcoming CD, I've taken a bit of a risk and am recording a few songs that have almost never been performed live due to the logistics of performing them solo (songs with a strong fiddle tune component) or simply because I've been flogging the already-recorded stuff when I've been touring and haven't had room in the set to try some of the new songs out.

With my producer, I also look at a balance of mood, subject, tempo, etc. Some songs will wait until the next recording because they don't fit the particular balance or they need more work.

Mae Moore: I have often found myself in a restaurant or somewhere where I hear a song or voice that sounds vaguely familiar but I can't place it. My husband usually leans over and says discreetly, "That's you". I rarely listen to my recordings after I make them...or when I do, it's years later and as with most things in life, some things I would have done differently but some things I am very proud of.

KJ Denhert: I love coming home with a new recording. Sometimes there's a brief period where I despise every last detail, like a post-partum depression. Then it's a good idea to put the song away for a few days. Most of the time yes, I can see an audience or a listener in my mind. But when I like something I have recorded it's the best feeling in the world.

Lorraine Hart: Everyone's probably most critical about their own instrument, their own performance, their own "sound" in the studio, where everything can be heard so well and intimately revisited, but time and experience get you less insecure about it. Years of making up set lists that flow certainly helps you choose songs for a CD that has legs, with natural pacing of different strides and keys. The studio "high" is way different than the live performance "high". In the live performance, an "off" something or other is lost in the travelling emotions of the performance, often unnoticed by most. Many fear or don't like the studio experience because mistakes show...but the beauty of that is the chance to make it right...to put the planets where you will in this galaxy you're building. Be willing to make the mistakes, learning from them and evolving through them, in the intimate privacy of rehearsals and studio work. That's the places for them. This builds a powerhouse of trusting yourself and your songs in live performance...the place where you want to get it right the first time.

Joanne Stacey: I remember being a kid and hearing my recorded voice on one of those old tape decks! Man, I hated that! But over the years, I have come to love my voice and rely on it to take me and my music to all the wonderful places it can go. When I am recording these days, I have learned that it is impossible for me to be objective about my performances and try and bring people I trust into the studio with me to keep me on track and to help bring out the best in me at the times when I want to just say " that's good enough!" I really love working in the studio and accept that while it is challenging, it is also immensely rewarding!

What does holding a good instrument feel like in your hands?

I love this question. It was sent to me by someone who doesn't play an instrument and she wanted to know how I felt about this. I love a good guitar. For the longest time I didn't know what a great instrument was. I could only afford cheap guitars and that's what I played. But over the years, I managed to get my hands on a few astonishing instruments, and I love the way they make me feel.

Sometimes I feel like I'm not good enough for the instrument I'm holding, like I don't know enough chords or patterns or whatever. But sometimes, they speak to me. They resonate with songs and ideas as soon as I touch them. That sounds so terribly cosmic, but it's true.

I met a man, Gary Norris, who is a luthier. He believes that every musician has an instrument that speaks to them alone. He's made it his mission in life to match the musician to the guitar much to the dismay of my pocketbook. Over the last few years, I've had the privilege to play and own some very fine guitars. I tend to outgrow instruments as I progress in my evolution. And Gary always finds the perfect one to replace the one I don't want anymore.

I feel connected to my music source when I play a great guitar. It talks to me and shares its melodies openly. Sometimes I have to coax it a little, but mostly it just is. It's like a part of my body.

I don't profess to be the greatest guitar player, but I've learned the value of a great instrument and it's a blessing indeed.

The Songwriter's Voice

Ian Thomas: One can often hear a million songs itching to get started when one sits behind a fabulous piano or a really well made and well-set up guitar.

Ed Winacott: I don't really think of myself as an instrumentalist at all....I tend to be more lyrically-driven in my songwriting. That being said, a fine instrument still has a feel to it...both a tone and an ease of use that draws me in and makes me better than I really am. Where does it resonate?...when it is all working, the way that I would describe the resonance is to use a mother holding child analogy....one unit not two things....the flesh of my flesh sort of thing....centered at the chest level but seeming to draw the other portions of me closer to that circle (not exactly clear I know but the best I can do).

David Essig: My first good guitar was a 1937 Martin D-18 that I still play. I got it when I was 19 and starting to write. Having said that, some of the most successful songs I've written in my head – driving or walking around – with no instrument at hand – just singing to myself. That's a good test of a good melody, by the way – that you can sing it to yourself without an instrument.

On recording your first CD...

I wrote an essay on recording a CD for a magazine once and I'd like to share it here; interesting in hindsight that I was only on CD #3 when I wrote this. Since then I've recorded three more. But these words still hold true.

1. Put together the very best packaging you can. You only have a very tiny window of time to attract a potential buyer and/or listener. Hire a graphics person, check, check and re-check your liner notes, lyrics, make it easy to read and easy to get around.

2. Work with the best producer and engineer you can. Even more so than that, work with people who get your sound and what you're trying to do. I produced our first CD and worked with Andrew Smith for the second. The difference is dramatic.

3. Stop worrying about the money. It's only money after all. Work out the details in advance as to how much you need to spend; then forget about it. You need to concentrate on getting the best sound you can that truly captures who and what you are.

4. Make a potential list of songs including about 5-6 more than you need and get everyone you know to listen and give you feedback. I listened to the order of my songs so many times I thought I'd go batty. But it's so important to take your listener on a journey with your CD.

5. Hire the best musicians you can. You know your best friend can play the bagpipes but wouldn't you rather have a professional who can give that extra bit only experience can give. It's so worth it to work with professionals.

6. Don't hire a producer or a studio just because they're expensive. Listen to what they've done and decide if that's the sound you want. I've seen too many

people hire very expensive producers and studios and end up with a product that is less than stellar.

7. Don't be afraid to record less. Nobody said the CD had to be 14 songs.

8. Talk to DJs, talk to venues, talk to people in the business. Do your homework in advance to see who's going to buy your CD; nothing more heart-wrenching than having 500 CDs in your basement that no one buys. (Ha, as of this date I think I have several hundred CDs in the storage locker; didn't listen to my own advice!)

9. Once you've completed the CD, forget about what it cost you. You have to move on. Be proud of what you've done and turn your creative energy to the next thing. It's so vital that you move on. It was one of the hardest things for me to do. I was certain I was going to take the folk world by storm.

10. Take that leap of faith. Believe with all your heart that you can do this. Than do it.

And repeat…

Chapter 21

Do you have any advice or words to share with others?

Do not be afraid to fail. Failure is as essential as succeeding. Without failure, we can't learn, without crap we can't know excellence. Be bold and brave, it is after all your art and your passion that appears, not anyone else's. We are all connected and all here for the same reasons. There is a great quote from C. S. Lewis that says...."every time you make a choice, you are turning the central part of you that chooses into something a little different from what it was before."[2]

Write from your heart and write honestly. Just start. Pick up the pen and start. It's that simple.

Shari Ulrich: Advice? As is so often said, write from what you know. Tell your own story, and don't let the inner critic inhibit you. No one else has your unique voice.

KJ Denhert: Be true to your inspiration. You'll enjoy what you do if that is your goal. If you want to make a living then study what you think defines success and try to create that. You'll have to probably strike some kind of balance between creativity and self-indulgence whether you realize it or not. So don't worry.

David Essig: If you've got the gift, use it in a way that speaks to the human condition with compassion and love. Emancipate yourself and your listeners as much as possible. And do it with a smile.

---

[2] Lewis, C.S. *Mere Christianity*, 1952

The Songwriter's Voice

Barry Mathers: My advice would be to listen to the great writers and see how they do it. Robbie Robertson has a story about Bob Dylan teaching him how to get from point A to C without going through B, meaning that you don't always have to be obvious about how you say something.

The first real song I wrote, "Play That Old Steel" is still one of my most favourite creations. I was so excited that I had written what I considered a good song and everyone I played it for agreed. I believe it was this song that inspired me to carry on as a writer.

Lorraine Hart: If you're asking what advice I'd give…here it is:

Love what you do and believe in yourself….but know that there's always more to learn and don't be afraid of your mistakes. As someone said, "For life to continue it only needs to reproduce itself….but for life to evolve, mistakes must be made."

Be willing to work hard, as in any job you'd want to do well at.

Don't settle for the easy rhyme and hackneyed lines…or get locked into the same old, same old chord changes. The challenge is to find new ways to say what humans have been feeling since they first began to howl at the moon in the year dot. Don't settle. Understand and accept that, like this oxymoronic existence, there will be great pain and great joy…and all the points in between. It's not the journey from here to a defined there; it's our lives of wandering and wonder. Be grateful. The gods struck us with their most beloved sickness…..and cure.

With my art I have made millions of dollars....worth of memories.....inside intimate moments with the Muse, with other musicians and with the audience. I've made a decent living doing what I love. I've made an indecent amount of love with the living I do.

One night after ending a show with a song I wrote about Manhattan and dreams, I felt pulled into the audience and began to greet the people I could reach. An elderly woman took my hand, pulling me down to where she could whisper in my ear.

"I grew up on that magic island," she said and with shiny eyes, she pressed my hand to her cheek, warm with her own memories.

That, my friend, is job satisfaction.

Yael Wand: There have been times when I am deep in doubt about my work as a performer and a songwriter, sometimes this happens when I want to be writing, or sometimes it's at the critical moment I have to get on stage. These are moments when there is no room for fear or questions. Once I can quiet my own demons, I found these times to be some of the most fulfilling and rewarding as a musician. I suppose it's when I'm at my lowest that the potential of sharing and making music is at its strongest, carrying the greatest power to transform.

It's easy to get caught up in writing for an audience or writing in a genre, but at the core I write for myself and I perform for the same reason, because I want to learn and understand and to transform myself. I strive to do the same for my audience and there's nothing as rewarding as knowing that I just might have done so with a song or with a killer performance.

At the times when I have given myself fully as a performer, when I have put complete faith into the act of performing, wonderful things return to me. It sounds cliché and silly but over and over again this is how good things come my way: new creative opportunities, new fans, new artistic insights, or just a joyful, elevating, irreplaceable experience between myself and an audience. In the face of my worst doubts as an artist I have walked on stage feeling utterly naked and vulnerable, done my job, and then walked off feeling completely renewed, wanting to do it all over again the next night.

Maria Dunn: Make sure you make time to play your instrument and sing and write songs. Don't burn out on the business stuff. There will always be too much of that to do it all.

Walking is a great way to clear your head, especially if you are a solo artist working from home. It's also a great way to get over writer's block and work on new ideas.

Joanne Stacey: I think if someone wanted to start writing songs, I would tell them to sit down and write out all the lyrics to their favourite songs longhand. See the similarities, notice the differences and understand the basics of a song. Next it would be meter and rhyming patterns. Break it down, understand it. Gain some understanding of how the melody needs to work with the words to evoke the feelings you want it to. There are so many ways to look at it but I think most people have to find their own way to that internal connection to spirit, for that is the essence of the song to me.

Mae Moore: If I were starting out as a songwriter today, I would look to those who came before me, who remained true to their art and craft, who have given us milestones in our lives and opened doors. Songwriters who have broken ground (Ani DiFranco), helped heal the world (John Lennon), shed light on the lives of others (Woody Guthrie) etc. Learn from the best and laugh with the rest. As long as the world spins, songwriters will be there to help point us in the right direction.

Ian Thomas: Most great songwriters have either got it or they don't and usually all of us have to find our own way. If you get great joy from songwriting it doesn't matter if it's good or bad. Let it out. Be prepared that others may love it, hate it, or could care less. C'est la vie.

AFTERWORD

I have always been attracted to the idea of community. We are only one small part of a greater tribe and it's our duty to develop and expand our community for the sake of survival and reproduction.

In all my years of being a songwriter, I have spent countless hours drawing other folks into the circle, getting them to open up and look at their own journeys, teaching them the value of letting others in, of allowing feedback and constructive criticism to help them grow.

Communities challenge and encourage their members. Without the interaction of outsiders, we would never experience chaos. And chaos promotes change and growth. It is essential to the community.

We all have tribes – family, close friends, associates, people who think like we do. But a tribe cannot be exclusive. It has to attract and deal with outsiders on a regular basis. And it's those very same outsiders that change us.

This book was my drawing together of the tribe, the tribe of songwriters. I wanted to include them in the conversations I've had in my head for years. I wanted to find out what made them desire to be songwriters. And I am so grateful that they answered the call. It's important for us to hear what others are doing, how they deal with the very same issues we all face.

I have seen the power of community. I have experienced the profound change a seemingly diverse group of strangers can bring about. I have felt the love that comes from being part of such a community. And it's changed me.

I don't live in a vacuum. I don't want to. I want my interactions with my fellow human beings to be open and honest. I want to share my desires, my pain, my joy and my challenges with as many folks as I can. It's why I write a blog. It's why I did this book.

It's enough to know that we are not alone. There are strangers who care about us. They can take the place of a dysfunctional family. They can provide the support and love we can't get anywhere else. And they do it without thought for themselves. Who wouldn't want that?

My friend, Lorraine gave me a great quote: "You are but one note on the songline of Man. Don't belittle the note and don't devour the line." Beautiful and I will add – this songline runs through us all. It connects us. It is our humanity.

Peace,
Jane Eamon
Kelowna, BC
August 2012

About the author

Jane Eamon, award-winning singer-songwriter-storyteller, has long captivated audiences with heartfelt songs exploring the frailties of human experience. Her debut book, *Caught in Time,* was a superb collection of song lyrics – some from her CD album of the same name, others from upcoming releases – along with revealing and thought-provoking selected poems.

With *The Songwriter's Voice*, Eamon delves deeper into the life and experiences of the songwriter – sharing her own thoughts and reflections and those of an array of fellow songwriters, including Ian Thomas, Shari Ulrich, Stephen Fearing, Mae Moore, David Essig and many more, in a unique book that is truly the first of its kind.

Jane Eamon resides in Kelowna, British Columbia, and divides her free time between book-signing events and live concerts. Visit her at Manor House: www.manor-house.biz

Manor House Publishing
905-648-2193
www.manor-house.biz